MW00711028

A Passion for
Christian Ministry
(A Primer For Young Preachers)

by

Lanis Kineman

Koinonia Associates
Knoxville, Tennessee

Copyright ©2013
Lanis Kineman
All rights Reserved.

No part of this publication may be reproduced, stored in a retrieval system, or transmitted in any form or by any means - electronic, mechanical, photocopy, recording, or otherwise - without receiving prior permission from the publishers.

ISBN 978-1-60658-025-7

Published by:
Koinonia Associates
7809 Timber Glow Trail
Knoxville, TN 37938

To learn how you can become a published author, visit
PublishwithKA.com
May 16, 2013

Cover photo by Michael Ralph.
Cover design by Darris Brock

Table of Contents

Chapter 1

ANSWERING THE CALL

Many books have been written embracing the high calling of the ministry of Jesus Christ. The challenges of such a calling are monumental and the consequences of each decision made may be the difference between success or failure. Jesus defined it and also modeled it for His followers. "If anyone would come after me, he must deny himself and take up his cross and follow me. For whoever wants to save his life will lose it, but whoever loses his life for me will find it." (Matthew 16:24,25). We're most familiar with his words "whoever wants to become great among you must be your servant, and whoever wants to be first must be slave of all. For even the Son of Man did not come to be served, but to serve, and to give his life as a ransom for many." (Mark 10:44,45). Jesus set the standard for those who would minister. He became the role model for the self-seeking apostles by washing their feet. The towel and basin have become symbols of servanthood.

The call to ministry may unfold through differing experiences. Allow me to share some of my own personal experiences that laid the groundwork for sixty-four years of ministry. It began with a Godly lady teacher of young men in a Sunday School Class in a small country church in Southern Illinois. She assigned each boy to teach the class on a given Sunday. Having emerged from a Presbyterian family background, I was drawn to the position of the Christian Church because of the adherence to Scriptural practices. Having been baptized in the Ohio river at the age of twelve, I began to search the Word. During my High School days, in the absence of a local pastor, I was asked to fill the pulpit on a few occasions. My first sermon was "Come and See" based upon Jesus response to two of the disciples who inquired of him, "Where are you staying?" to which Jesus replied, "Come and you will see." (John 1:39). The result was their spending the day with him . The church was packed with curious townspeople who wanted to hear what a young teenager had to say. The Summer following my sophomore year of High School I attended a week of Christian Service Camp held in Dixon Springs State Park in Southern Illinois. Following my Junior Year I was asked to return to Senior Youth Week to teach a class which introduced me to one of the most influential gatherings for recruiting youth for specialized Christian Service. Christian Service Camps continued to be a major recruiting ministry for many years. Though every Christian in the church has both a privilege and responsibility to carry out the Great Commission, specialized ministry has been urgently needed as the apostle Paul set forth in Ephesians 4:11-13.

Many evangelists and music ministers led revivals in my home church, who in turn inspired me to be an ambassador for the Lord. Upon graduation from High School, I was invited by the Minister, L. L. Chamness to spend my Summer in Hammond, Indiana working for a construction firm during the day and doing office work in the evening. On weekends I was privileged to work with the young people.

Having been informed about Johnson Bible College in Knoxville, Tn., by J. B. Smith, song evangelist, I decided to enroll the Fall of 1944. Accompanied by my good friend, Gene Dye, we traveled by bus and showed up at the Registrar's office for enrollment. Without financial means for a College education, I worked fifteen hours a week in the kitchen, carried fifteen hours of study and during my Senior year was asked by Dr. R. M. Bell to teach a typing class in the evening for other students. During my Junior year, I traveled by train to Shepherdsville, Ky. to preach on Sunday at the Christian Church. The leadership finally decided that the weekly transportation to the Church was costing me more than they were paying me so I was given a small increase in salary to cover travel expenses by train each weekend.

Having spent my Summer in Shepherdsville following my Junior year at College, was an invaluable experience. Responding to an ad in the CHRISTIAN STANDARD of the opening for a minister in Mt. Vernon, Ky., I was selected to be their next Minister. I continued my week-end travel to Kentucky. Graduating from College on May 31, 1948, my wife to be, Kathryn Turnbull and I, were two of only seven graduates of the class of '48. We traveled by bus to Paterson, N. J. where Kathryn was ordained by her preacher father on Wednesday, June 2, and we exchanged marriage vows in a large church wedding on Saturday, June 5, 1948.

We returned to Mt. Vernon, Ky. where we continued ministry at the church until 1951. In that year our first son, Larry, was born in Richmond, Kentucky. We resigned to accept a call to the Normanda Christian Church,

Tipton, Indiana. While ministering there, I completed my graduate work at Butler University School of Religion, now Christian Theological Seminary, for my Master of Divinity degree, August 3. 1956.

After six years of numerical growth and building expansion, we accepted a call to the Carlisle Christian Church in Carlisle, Kentucky, following the retirement of J. J. Whitehouse. For my degree at Butler I chose to do my dissertation on "Barton Stone's Concept of the Holy Spirit." I was not to foresee that I would be called to minister at the historic church that Stone helped to establish in 1820. The five years there were to have a major impact upon the direction of my ministry over forthcoming years. Some of these experiences will be treated in another chapter.

The Bible is replete with the call of prophets, apostles and preachers who answered the call for proclaiming the message of the Lord and the nature of that response. God chose Noah to carry his warning of earth's destructive flood to an evil and vile generation. Noah responded to the call to construct an ark, of exact dimensions. for the survival of himself and seven other members of his family. He became the first preacher of righteousness in the history of mankind.

The history of mankind may be spelled out in the rearranging of four letters in the Bible. **L-I-V-E.** When Adam and Eve were created, they were designed in nature to **LIVE** in perfect fellowship with God. However, they chose **EVIL** in their disobedience to God. . Then men became **VILE** in all of their ways. . With the coming and death of Christ, the **VEIL** in the Temple that symbolically separated God from man was removed at the hour of his death on the cross. Thus, the death and resurrection of Christ paved the way for man to **LIVE** again. We have the account throughout Biblical history of God raising up spokesmen to carry out His message to the people.

Noah., a preacher of righteousness in the midst of a rebellious generation, was instructed to build an ark for the survival of himself and his family prior to the flood that wiped out mankind from the earth.

In time, Moses was born and miraculously survived the death decree in Egypt and was providentially cared for in Pharaoh's household. In his adulthood he chose to identify with his own people and became their deliverer from oppression in Egypt. Moses was recruited through the means of a burning bush in the wilderness . He was reluctant to accept the role but God overcame his fears of inadequacy and excuse-making and sent him to be the Deliverer of Israel.

The prophet Jeremiah relates his call to prophesy when the people of Jerusalem went into exile. "The word of the Lord came to me, saying,

7

'Before I formed you in the womb I knew you, before you were born I set you apart; I appointed you as a prophet to the nations.' The Lord overcame his reluctance with the assurance of His presence and power. (Jeremiah 1:4-10).

Isaiah the prophet's call came in a year of transition (the death of King Uzziah) as a result of an overwhelming experience in the temple. (Isaiah 6).

Turning to the New Testament, we have the Great Commission of Jesus prior to his ascension. He, who embodied ministry in its fullness, called and instructed his followers to implement his plan. His words are clearly stated: "All authority in heaven and on earth has been given to me. Therefore go and make disciples of all nations, baptizing them in the name of the Father and of the Son and of the Holy Spirit, and teaching them to obey everything I have commanded you. And surely I will be with you always, to the very end of the age." (Matthew 28:18-20).

In fulfilling the Great Commission, we have the authority of Christ himself behind the command. By accepting the call with the assurance of Jesus' plan and presence, there are at least five conditions relating to accepting the challenge:

A. ORIENTATION. Faith is the foundation of accepting the challenge. The only definition of faith that we have in the Scripture is Hebrews 11:1 (KJV). The writer defines it as follows: "Now faith is the substance of things hope for, the evidence of things not seen." Thus, sub-stance translates to "stand under our hope." Hope, in turn, consists of both "desire" and "reasonable expectation". I may hope for something but it must be based upon reliable promises. The writer proceeds to enumerate a long list of the faithful who did not personally receive in their lifetime the fulfillment of their hopes but, none the less , their faith was translated into positive action. The chapter concludes with the following statement: "And these all, having obtained a good report through faith, received not the promise: God having provided some better thing for us, that they without us should not be made perfect." ((11:39,40).

B. MOTIVATION---The reason for accepting the call must be implacable. The call to the Christian ministry must not be based upon flippant motivation or for lucrative gain. like the preacher who was questioned about his motivation and explained that he saw P.C. written in the sky, instructing him to Preach Christ. Those who had been listening to his preaching retorted that he misunderstood the message. It really meant "Plow corn." The apostle Paul set the standard high in his resolve to proclaim Christ, when he wrote: "But what things were gain to me, those I counted loss for Christ. Yea doubtless, and I count all things but loss for the excellency of the knowledge of Christ Jesus my Lord: for whom I have suffered the loss of all things, and do count them but dung, that I may win Christ." (Philippians 3:7-8)

When I enrolled at Johnson Bible College in 1944, I was impressed with the statement carved in stone at the entrance to the Main Building which read: "Open day and night to the young man desiring above every other desire to preach the gospel of Jesus Christ." I was also impressed with the challenge by President R. M. Bell to the Freshman students: "If anyone of you desire to do anything other than to preach the gospel, pack your suitcase and leave the campus now."

C. DEDICATION–Writing to the church at Corinth, Paul sets forth the nature of ministry to which we are called. "But thanks be to God, who always leads us in triumphal procession in Christ and through us spreads everywhere the fragrance of the knowledge of him. For we are to God the aroma of Christ among those who are being saved and those who are perishing. To the one we are the smell of death; to the other, the fragrance of life. And who is equal to such a task? Unlike so many we do not peddle the word of God for profit. On the contrary, in Christ, we speak before God with sincerity, like men sent from God."–(2 Cor. 2:14-17).

D. PROCLAMATION–Paul admonishes young Timothy with the following instruction: "Preach the Word; be prepared in season and out of season; correct, rebuke encourage–with great patience and careful instruction. For the time will come when men will not put up with sound doctrine. Instead, to suit their own desires, they will gather around them a great number of teachers to say what their itching ears want to hear. They will turn their ears away from the truth and turn aside to myths .But you, keep your head in all situations, endure hardship, do the work of an evangelist, discharge all the duties of your ministry."(2 Timothy 4:2-5).

E. EXPECTATION–The closing statement of our Lord's commission is: "And surely I will be with you always, to the very end of the age." (Matt. 28:20).

The Apostle Paul, near the time for his departure from this earthly life declared of his own ministry: "I have fought the good fight, I have finished the race, I have kept the faith. ;Now there is in store for me the crown of righteousness, which the Lord, the righteous Judge, will award to me on that day–and not only to me, but also to all who have longed for his appearing." (2 Timothy 4:7,8).

Again Paul, in his letter to the church at Rome, brings the urgency of the call to ministry into sharp focus when he writes:"The word is near you; it is in your mouth and in your heart, that is, the word of faith we are proclaiming: That if you confess with your mouth, Jesus is Lord, and believe in your heart that God raised him from the dead, you will be saved. For it is with your heart that you believe and are justified, and it is with your mouth that you confess and are saved." As the Scripture says, "Everyone who trusts in him will never be put to shame. . . . Everyone who calls on the name of the Lord will be saved." How, then, can they call on the one they have not believed in? And how can they believe in the one of whom they have not heard? And how can they hear without someone preaching to them? And how shall they preach unless they are sent? As it is written, ' How beautiful are the feet of those who bring good news!'"

The Bible has been described as containing Basic Information Before Leaving Earth.

An admonition in the second letter to Timothy speaks volumes:

"Preach the Word; be prepared in season and out of season; correct, rebuke and encourage–with great patience and careful instruction. For the time will come when men will not put up with sound doctrine. Instead, to suit their own desires, they will gather around them a great number of teachers to say what their itching ears want to hear. They will turn their ears away from the truth and turn aside to myths. But you, keep your head in all situations, endure hardship, do the work of an evangelist, discharge all the duties of your ministry." (2 Timothy 4:2-5)

The Lord does not call us to ministry to be popular; rather to be faithful to His Word.

"Only one life will soon be past;
Only what's done for Christ will last."

The Bible speaks of many individuals who made excuses for not responding to God's call to leadership: Moses, Jonah and Jeremiah are but a few. If any have excuses for not heeding the Lord's call, consider the following:

LET THE BIBLE REMOVE OUR EXCUSES!

"I CAN'T."
"I can do all things through Christ who strengthens me" (Philippians 4:13)

"I HAVEN'T TIME."
"Seek ye first the kingdom of God . . . ." (Matthew 6:33).

"GET SOMEONE ELSE."
"Here am I, send me." (Isaiah 6:8)

"IT CAN'T BE DONE."
"With God all things are possible." (Mark 10:27)

"I AM TOO TIRED."
"They who wait for the Lord will gain new strength." (Isa.40:30)

"I WILL SOME OTHER TIME."
"Now is the accepted time." (2 Cor. 6:2)

"I KNOW I OUGHT TO, BUT."
"To him who knows to do good and does it not: to him it is sin." (James 4:17)

"I MAY FAIL."
"Lo, I am with you always, even to the end of the world." (Matt. 28:20)

"I DON'T LIKE TO."
"For even Christ pleased not himself." (Romans 15:3)

"I NEGLECTED IT."
"How shall we escape if we neglect . . . ." (Hebrews 2:3)

"LET THEM HELP THEMSELVES."
"Bear ye one another's burdens and so fulfill the law of Christ."(Galatians 6:2)

Hebrews, chapter 11, speaks of the long list of heroes of the Faith: Abel, Enoch, Noah, Abraham, Isaac, Jacob, Sara, Jacob, Joseph, Moses, Rahab, Gideon, Barak, Samson, Jephthah, David and Samuel. The writer sums it up by saying that they "through faith subdued kingdoms, wrought righteousness, obtained promises, stopped the mouths of lions, quenched the violence of fire, escaped the edge of the sword, out of weakness were made strong, waxed valiant in fight, turned to flight the armies of the aliens (Heb. 11:33-34).

To put it into the proper perspective, we could sum it up as follows:

1. BY FAITH THEY DID THE IMPOSSIBLE.
2. BY FAITH THEY SAW THE INVISIBLE.
3. BY FAITH THEY BELONGED TO THE COMPANY OF THE ACCOUNTABLE.
4. BY FAITH THEY BECAME THE INVALUABLE.

HOW TO BE EFFECTIVE AFTER RECEIVING THE CALL TO MINISTRY!

I. First of all, there must be a personal commitment to Christ and a desire above every other desire to preach the gospel. (1 Cor. 2:2)

II. There must be a willingness to spend time in the Scriptures, do necessary research and fully understand the nature of the Church for which Jesus died. (1 Cor. 12:12-20). "Jesus came to pay a debt He didn't owe because we owed a debt we couldn't pay."

III. Live a life daily before all people that will be an example for all believers. "For he hath made him to be sin for us, who knew no sin: that we might be made the righteousness of God in him."(2 Cor. 5:21).

IV. Demonstrate love for all people for whom Christ died. Jesus said, "Thou shalt love the Lord thy God with all thy heart, and with all thy soul, and with all thy mind. This is the first and great commandment. And the second is like unto it, Thou shalt love thy neighbour as thyself." (Matthew 22:37-39).

V. Don't equate separation from the world with isolationism. We must be in the world but not of the world. For a boat to serve its purpose, it must be in the water, but when the water is in the boat it's purpose is defeated.

VI. Have faith in the power of Christ in your life. "Greater is he that is in you than he that is in the world."(1 John 4:4).

VII. Don't let personal pride of being rejected by men discourage you from witnessing to your faith. Jesus was rejected by the very ones who should have received him. The apostle Paul encountered opposition and rejection in Athens but continued to proclaim Christ as Lord. In the end, some believed.

VIII. Don't be judgmental in your attitude and erect barriers. Jesus dined in the house of sinners and won them as his followers.

IX. Cultivate a genuine love for persons in need. Jesus was never class conscious in his ministry but rather was completely color blind. Socially, our outreach is to both the down-and- outers and also the up-and-outers.

Chapter 2

PROFILE OF A LEADER

The preacher is called upon to wear many different hats in carrying out endless responsibilities. In doing so he might find it easier to do the work of ten men rather than train ten to share the work load But to equip others to share ministries benefits the whole church.

This principle of leadership dates back to the account of Moses leading the Israelites out of Egyptian bondage. When Jethro, Moses' father-in-law, observed the overwhelming task of Moses presiding over the people from day to night, he admonished him:

"What you are doing is not good. You and these people who come to you will only wear yourselves out. The work is too heavy for you; you cannot handle it alone. Listen now to me and I will give you some advice, and may God be with you. You must be the people's representative before God and bring their disputes to him. Teach them the decrees and laws, and show them the way to live and the duties they are to perform. But select capable men from all the people–men who fear God, trustworthy men who hate dishonest gain–and appoint them as officials over thousands, hundreds, fifties and tens. Have them serve as judges for the people at all times, but have them bring every difficult case to you; the simple cases they can decide themselves. That will make your load lighter, because they will share it with you. If you do this and God so commands, you will be able to stand the strain, and all these people will go home satisfied." (Exodus 18:17-23).

This could be the first example of an EQUIPPING MINISTRY for leading others.

During the 1970s and 1980s in my ministry at the Bethany Christian Church in Anderson Indiana I led seminars on Church Leadership and

Church Growth throughout the Midwest. One unresolved issue was what title should be appropriate for the local pastor. The responses covered a wide range–elder, evangelist, pastor, reverend, preacher and leader. In the final analysis, my opinion was not the title but rather the ministry performed .that was most important. As the old expression goes–"The proof of the pudding is in the eating." The book of Acts gives us the first insight into leadership in the Church.

What we do know is that Luke records in Acts 6 the appointment of seven men in the Jerusalem church to serve the needs of widows who were being neglected. When the apostle Paul writes to Titus about unfinished matters in Crete, he is instructed to ordain elders in every town. He proceeds to list both the positive as well as the negative attributes of those who serve. (Titus 1:7-9). Writing to young Timothy he emphasizes the congregation's obligation to those who lead and the responsibility of the leader:

To the scattered church, Peter writes :

"To the elders among you, I appeal as a fellow elder, a witness of Christ's sufferings and one who also will share in the glory to be revealed: Be shepherds of God's flock that is under your care, serving as overseers–not because you must, but because you are willing, as God wants you to be; not greedy for money, but eager to serve; not lording it over those entrusted to you, but being examples to the flock. And when the Chief Shepherd appears, you will receive the crown of glory that will never fade away." (1 Peter 5:1-4).

The bottom line to whatever title the leader may be given, is to under stand that leadership must be translated into servanthood. Jesus' response to the request of James and John for the right and left hand positions in His kingdom was "... whoever wants to become great among you must be your servant, and whoever wants to be first must be slave of all. For even the Son of Man did not come to be served, but to serve and to give his life as a ransom for many." (Mark 10:43-45).

In my own ministry in years past, the men selected by the church to serve as Deacons were given the opportunity to choose one of many areas of service within the church who in turn reported back to the Eldership.

In many New Testament Churches in the twenty-first century the office of deacon has been replaced with Ministry leaders.

The Responsible leaders will, first and foremost, be found faithful both to the Scriptures as well as to their responsibilities. To use the words of

John Mohr:

"O may all who come behind us find us faithful;
May the fire of our devotion light their way;
May the footprints that we leave, lead them to believe;
And the lives we live inspire them to obey.
O may all who come behind us find us faithful."

"But in your hearts set apart Christ as Lord. Always be prepared to give an answer to everyone who asks you to give the reason for the hope that you have. But do this with gentleness and respect, keeping a clear conscience, so that those who speak maliciously against your good behavior in Christ may be ashamed of their slander." (1 Peter 3:15,16)

L. Palmer Young, in a workshop on leadership at the North American Christian Convention in 1977, set forth the following relative to the minister in the pulpit as a leader:

1. "Ministry in general is always total service of the total Christian community, whether in relation to its own members or to others
2. "Any kind of ministry, however, should be organized to some degree, so that leadership can be effectively utilized."
3. "Leadership should usually be according to competence–the culmination of abilities that can best get the job accomplished."

Myron Taylor has offered excellent advice relative to the preacher's sermons:

Preaching should be Biblical.
Preaching should be Christ Centered.
Preaching should be relevant to the needs of the people.
Preaching should be positive (good news). "Not what the world
    is coming to but who has come to the world"
Preaching should be done with faith, love and clarity.
The delivery should be interesting. Otherwise, minds will
    wander.
Preaching should be encouraging. Hope for the hopeless; Faith
    for the doubter; Love for the lonely.

"LEADERSHIP WORKS IN AN OPERATING ROOM, NOT A BUTCHER SHOP. THE INSTRUMENT OF CHOICE IS A SCALPEL, NOT A MEAT CLEAVER."
MAXIMS # 480 –*Dr. Paul Benjamin*

James A. Cress, in an article titled: "HOW TO DESTROY YOUR LEADERSHIP," offers the following advice: "Experience, then teach the impact of the gospel in your daily life and work: The following negatives in leadership were evaluated in a committee meeting:

1. LACK of CREDIBILITY. When leaders act differently than their expressed values, people lose confidence....Situational leadership must never mean situational ethics.

2. INCOMPETENCE. Too often settling for mediocre rather than excellence.

3. LACK of VISION. The lack of vision in not preparing for the future.

4. SELF-SERVICE. Self seeking rather than servant leadership.

5. OVER EXTENSION. Concentrating on endless emergencies while ignoring the important.

6. EXCLUSIVITY. Avoid the trap of listening only to those who comprise your inner circle.

7. CRONYISM. Job criteria should never be previous proximity to the leader. Solicit input from critics.

8. LACK of COMMON SENSE: Ask, will it work? Seek counsel. Demand scrutiny.

9. FAILURE to INTEGRATE FAITH & LIFE: . If Faith does not impact performance of my vocation, I am not truly a believer.

SERVANT LEADERSHIP DEFINED
(See Acts 20:17-35)

In a confrontation with the Scribes and Pharisees, Jesus rebuked them for their ostentatious conduct and proceeded to challenge their use of self-imposed titles:

"But be not ye called Rabbi: for one is your Master, even Christ; and all ye are brethren. And call no man your father upon the earth: for one is your Father, which is in heaven. Neither be ye called masters: for one is your Master, even Christ. But he that is greatest among you shall be your SERVANT. And whosoever shall exalt himself shall be abased; and he that shall humble himself shall be exalted." (Matthew 23:8-12).

We do the humbling and God does the exalting. As leaders, our authority is not positional, but rather earned by our attitude and conduct.

In James 4:10 the same admonition is given. "Humble yourselves in the sight of the Lord, and he shall lift you up." In verse 7 & 8 he gives a twofold action: "Resist the Devil" and "Draw near to God" and He will draw nigh to you. In Mark 10:42-45 Jesus says, "Whosoever will be great among you, shall be your minister: and whosoever of you will be the chiefest, shall be servant of all. "Servanthood and leadership are not contradictions but compatible in Jesus' teaching on leadership. The terms manager and leader are frequently used as synonyms. However, it should be noted that every manager needs to be a leader, but not every leader needs to be a manager. Leader comes first: Leadership captures concepts, visions and overall direction. Once these are established, management sees that it is done.

RICHARD HUTCHESON explains leadership as "a function of the relationship between persons, those in charge and those who voluntarily follow. Leadership both shapes and is shaped by those who follow. The one thing it cannot do is ignore the constituency."

ROBERT RUSSELL weighs in on the role of a leader in recommending the following way effective leaders do the following:

> 1. Confront, without delay, real problems within the membership: False doctrine, open immorality of members, and a divisive spirit in attitude,
> 2. Exercise reasonable flexibility in matters of opinion.
> 3. Manifest open support of equipping ministers.
> 4. Delegate responsibility and Exercise a faith that is willing to take risks.

PETER WAGNER: "An equipper is a leader who actively sets goals for a congregation according to the will of God, obtains goal ownership from the people and sees that each church member is properly motivated and equipped to do his or her part in accomplishing the goals."

WITHOUT RESPECT FOR LEADERS BY THOSE BEING LED, ANARCHY, CHAOS AND CONFUSION will result within the church.

WINSTON CHURCHILL: "Leadership is the capacity and will to rally men and women to a common cause and the character which inspires confidence."

APOSTLE PAUL'S EXAMPLE: He modeled the Christian life by his example in teaching faithfully publicly and privately the essentials of the faith and declared the full counsel of God: (Acts 20:17-32)

Be personally prepared: Know the Word. Understand the responsibilities of the office: ABILITY, RESPONSIBILITY, AVAILABILITY & ACCOUNTABILITY are equally important.

Be People Oriented. (vs. 28) Jesus said, "I am the Good Shepherd and my sheep know me" (John 10:14) There is the danger of putting policy before people; management over ministry.

Be Divinely Directed. (vs. 28).The Holy Spirit has made you overseers. Oversee means to look upon, or take care of. The Holy Spirit. provides the spiritual gifts of leaders, prepares the man and directs in the selection process.

The inevitable question must be raised: "Where does strong leadership come from?"

My own experience over sixty-four years of the located ministry has taught me the following:

Leadership is <u>earned</u>. The productive years of a given pastorate usually begins around the fourth, fifth or sixth year. It takes time to earn the right to lead by demonstrating servanthood.

Leadership is <u>discerned.</u> The gift of faith and leadership. The gift of God to discern with extraordinary confidence the will and purpose of God for the future of His work. The gift of leadership is set forth in Romans 12:8 and 1 Cor. 12:9.

Leadership is further <u>learned</u>. The gift needs to be developed through books, tapes, seminars, experience, etc.

When the apostle Paul wrote his letter to the church at Philippi, he confessed his need to press on in his pursuit for sharing the gospel.

He wrote: "Brethren, I count not myself to have apprehended: but this *one thing I do*, forgetting those things which are behind, and reaching forth unto those things which are before, I press toward the mark for the prize of the high calling of God in Christ Jesus." (Philippians 3:13,14). His philosophy was not to major in minors but rather make **CONCENTRATION** a priority.

I like the slogan stated a few years ago by the Eastside Christian Church in Fullerton, Ca. .which stated " The main thing is to keep the main thing the main thing."

There's an old story about a farmer who one morning decided to plow the south forty. His tractor needed greasing, so he started for the barn to get grease, but on the way he noticed that the pigs hadn't been fed. Near the corn crib was a pile of sacks, reminding him that the potatoes were sprouting. On the way to the potato pit, he passed the woodpile and remembered that the kitchen stove was burning low. While picking up the wood, he saw that one of his chickens was ailing, so he dropped the wood to doctor the chicken...and so it went to the end of the day and he still hadn't greased the tractor or plowed the south field. This story mirrors the experience of many of us and should cause us to examine our priorities.

Some valid questions should be entertained. Do we have grand visions of great service that never gets done?

Have we found too many other things to do that interfere with our goal of being a productive servant in the Lord's Kingdom? The farmer in the story didn't have any priorities. He just flowed with the tide of events confronting him. Our lives contain plenty of pigs to feed, wood to cut and chickens to gather; however, we dare not allow them to get in our way of doing the main thing. The Lord has given us a job to do, and He has and He will enable us to do it IF we make His will our priority.

Our ministry daily produces many things to be done and we must decide on the priorities. In my own experience, I made a list of things that needed to be done each day and then selected the most challenging first to be done. This enabled me to performs the other tasks with peace of mind and a sense of accomplishment for the day.

After sorting out our priorities, the obvious next step is **COMMITMENT.** As leaders we cannot lead where we will not go and we cannot teach what we do not know. Jesus said,"My food is to do the will of him who sent me and to finish his work . . . even now the fields are ripe unto the harvest . . . (John 4:34,35).

Paul admonished young Timothy: "Fan into flame the gift of God, which is in you through the laying on of hands. For God did not give us a spirit of timidity, but a spirit of power, of love and of self-discipline. So don't be ashamed to testify about our Lord . . ." (2 Timothy 1:6,7).

That spiritual commitment does not take the form of spiritual hermits isolated in our high tech offices addressing all the problems from our computers, telephones and intercoms.

John Henry Newman said it best:

> "I sought to hear the voice of God
> And climbed the topmost steeple;
> But God declared, 'Go down again'
> I dwell among the people"

COMPASSION is feeling while doing. Jesus wept over Jerusalem, the city of the Jewish Ecclesiastical establishment: "O Jerusalem, Jerusalem, you who kill the prophets and stone those sent to you, how often I have longed to gather your children together as a hen gathers her chicks under her wings, but you were not willing." (Matt. 23:37).

How many sleepless nights have we had recently over the lost in our cities in both high and low places, who if they died tonight, would be in

Christless graves? Our love and concern along with our own struggles to focus our faith must be transparent. This will break down the barriers and bridge the gap between the minister and congregation. The future will present a greater challenge in motivating people for ministry. The most significant resource in people's lives in the twenty-first century will no longer be MONEY but TIME. The quality of programs and projects must be excellent and the purpose well defined. Jesus said, "NOT EVERYONE WHO SAYS TO ME 'LORD, LORD,' WILL ENTER THE KINGDOM ;OF HEAVEN, BUT ONLY HE WHO DOES THE WILL OF MY FATHER IN HEAVEN." (Matthew 7:21). This is heavy stuff! In Matthew 22 we read about a Pharisee who was an authority on the Law testing Jesus:. "Which is the greatest commandment in the Law?" Jesus replied, "Love the Lord your God with all your heart, and with all your soul and with all your mind. This is the first and greatest command. Second is like it: "Love your neighbor as yourself. All the Law and the Prophets hang on these two commandments." (Matthew 22:37-40).

LOVE MUST BE EXPRESSED THROUGH THE HAND, THE HEART AND THE HEAD. We spell it M-I-N-I-S-T-R-Y.

Outside of Christ Himself, the person who best modeled this was Barnabas. He was an encourager. While Paul was a dynamic preacher, it was Barnabas, his companion in ministry, with his generous attitude and selfless behavior, enabled Paul to impact what he did. Barnabas was a role-model of generosity that we would do well to emulate.

BARNABAS WAS A MAN WITH A GENEROUS HAND

(Acts 4:33-37)

We first learn about Barnabas in the Jerusalem Church where in the fellowship of believers, no Christian was content with his own possessions while others within the fellowship had needs. He is singled out as selling a piece of property and giving the proceeds to the common treasury. His example prompted others to do the same, some from the right motive but others from a selfish motive. Ananias and Sapphira gave for the wrong reasons and were struck dead. The believers had all things in common, not because the system demanded it, but because there was a willingness to share what they had. Barnabas was a Levite, of the Priestly tribe of Israel. Under the Old Testament system the Law forbad them from acquiring real estate but that prohibition was later abolished. He owned property and his gift was obviously from the sale of property he had owned. His example was not unlike the widow's mite, who gave all she had.

BARNABAS WAS A MAN WITH A GENEROUS HEAD

(Acts 9:26,27)

A man who has a generous hand does not always have a generous head. The wealthy giver tends to be self-important and vulnerable to flattery. Anything out of his accustomed line of thought is suspect and frowned upon. It is to Barnabas' credit that he not only had an open hand but an open mind as well. Saul the persecutor of Christians came to Jerusalem after three years without letter of commendation following his conversion and was not received with open arms by the brethren. Barnabas stuck his neck out and commended Paul to Peter and James as a Christian brother. He admonished them not to let their prejudices mar a chosen vessel of the Holy Spirit. He was also the key to building trust between Jerusalem and Antioch. He was the good-will ambassador sent by the Jerusalem Church to check out the strange happenings at Antioch. He chose Paul to go with him and together they spent a whole year teaching and encouraging new Christians at Antioch.

BARNABAS POSSESSED A GENEROUS HEART

(Acts 13:l; 35:35-40)

Barnabas was willing to make allowances for the weaknesses of mortal man. The most painful experience of Barnabas, I'm sure, was his sharp difference with his good and trusted friend, Paul, over the treatment of John Mark On the first Missionary journey, Barnabas had taken so prominent a place that the Lystrians called him "The King of the gods" while Paul was referred to as his chief spokesman. Mark, who accompanied them, who was possibly a pampered child from an affluent home, became homesick and deserted them on their journey. Barnabas stood up for Mark, feeling that though he failed once, he should be given a second chance. Paul was strongly opposed to taking him on their Second Missionary Journey, because of the first episode. So, they parted company, each choosing separate partners: Barnabas with Mark and Paul with Silas. Barnabas took Mark to his home territory, Cyprus, where tradition says he labored faithfully till he died. 2 Timothy 4:11 gives us insight that Barnabas had more heart than Paul. However, from the Prison in Rome, Paul wrote to Timothy: "Only Luke is with me. Take Mark and bring him with thee; for he is profitable for me for the ministry. It is to Paul's credit that he forgave Mark and recognized his ability to make good in ministry. Barnabas was a champion of fairness *The next chapter will examine how the Minister relates to staff, elders and other leaders within the congregation.*

Chapter 3

DEVELOPING A CARING LEADERSHIP

I. A CARING LEADERSHIP IS DEVELOPED WHEN EACH ONE HAS AN UNDERSTANDING OF WHAT IS EXPECTED OF HIM. (Acts 20:28-32; 1 Timothy 3:1-7; Titus 1:5-16; 1 Peter 1:5-11).

   A. Feed the flock. (Acts 20:28; 1 Timothy 3:2).
   B. Shepherd the flock (1 Peter 5:2; Titus 1:9).
   C. Examples to the flock (1 Peter 5:3).
       1. Lead by example in humility.
       2. Not being tough and dictatorial but compassionate and giving.

II. A CARING LEADERSHIP BEGINS WITH A PROPER UNDERSTANDING OF THE FELLOWSHIP OF THE CHURCH. (1 John 1:1-7; Acts 2:42).

   A. Three Options:
       1. Individualism fosters anarchy and division.
       2. Institutionalism exploits and results often in apathy or rebellion.
       3. *Koinonia* translates into Sharing.
   B. Fellowship hinges upon our acceptance of Christ's Lordship and the surrender of our will to the will of Christ.

"Fellowship of the Spirit is not something that we extend or withdraw. It is something we share. Our task is not to grant it but to guard it in the bond of peace. Fellowship is a state entered by responding to the call of God. 'God is faithful, by whom you were called into the fellowship of His Son, Jesus Christ.' (1 Cor. 1:9). Everyone who hears the call of God and answers it is in the fellowship...by the grace of God. It is the invisible principle which joins every member in a working relationship. It is a gift to the church and not a gift of it. Fellowship in Christ is not contingent upon being right on every point of doctrine...It is not the result of each being perfect, but of each being in the Perfect One. One can be in Jesus and be mistaken about many things." --Carl Ketcherside in the MISSION MESSENGER, Feb., 1972.

III. CARING LEADERSHIP DEPENDS UPON THE IMPLEMENTATION OF A SELECTION PROCESS THAT IS ROOTED IN SCRIPTURE. (Acts 6:3,4; Titus 1:5) The procedure followed while I was Minister at Bethany Christian Church, Anderson, Indiana, was as follows:

   A. Recommendation of candidates by a Nominating Committee.
   B. Screening of the recommendations by the current eldership.
   C. Personal interviews with potential candidates.
   D. Selection by ballot by the congregation.
   E. Term of office established (Not a lifetime position).

IV. CARING LEADERSHIP IS DEVELOPED WHERE EACH PERSON IS EXPECTED TO GIVE ACCOUNTABILITY TO SOME OVERSEER.

   A. Properly discern ability of each leader (Ephesians 4:11-16).
   B. Delegate responsibility in caring for the flock and in directing ministries. (1 Cor. 12:14-27).
   C. Expect accountability from functioning committees.
   D. Encourage availability of spiritual leaders.
   E. Maintain flexibility in carrying out programs.

V. CARING LEADERSHIP IS DEVELOPED WHEN EACH LEADER RECOGNIZES THE DIFFERENCE BETWEEN AUTHORITY AND AUTHORITARIANISM.

   A. Authority and authoritarianism should not be confused. The second says: "This is right because I say so." The first says "I say this because it is right." A good leader has authority on his side but he is not authoritarian" – Joe Ellis in "THE CHURCH ON PURPOSE."
   B. Spiritual oversight is based upon the Word of God, not human opinion. (1 Timothy 5:17).
   C. Leaders must earn authority by their Christian example–not positional authority granted by the office. Respect is earned by commitment, consistency and concern for the members of the Fellowship.
   D. Leaders will discipline their men within the ranks and members

of the Fellowship. (Hebrews 13:7,17).

1. Person
   a. Withdraw fellowship from one who spreads false doctrine. (2 Thess. 4:14,15)
   b. Withdraw from members practicing immorality openly. (1 Cor. 5:1-5).
   c. Withdraw from those with divisive spirits and attitudes. (Titus 3:10,11; Romans 15:17; Jude 15-19).
   d. Withdraw from those who are idle when able to work and when work is available (2Thess. 3:6-15).
2. Purpose is to save the person, not to destroy him. (1 Cor. 5:5). To prevent the leavening effect which can affect the whole body (1 Cor. 5:6,7)
3. Procedure: Go to the erring brother or sister in private. (Matthew 18:15-17). If he will not repent, take two or three witnesses;. If he will not listen, take it to the church, then withdraw fellowship.

VI. CARING LEADERSHIP DEPENDS UPON A RIGHTFUL UNDERSTANDING OF WHAT IT MEANS TO HAVE THE SPIRIT OF CHRIST. (Philippians 2:5-8)

A. Characteristics of that Spirit:
   1. Spirit of humility, meekness & gentleness (Philippians 2:5-8)
   2. Spirit of kindness and compassion. (Matthew 9:36)
   3. Spirit of mercy and forgiveness toward the erring. (John 8:11)
   4. Spirit of unswerving obedience to the will of God (Matthew 3:5).
   5. Spirit of fidelity to the truth of God's revelation. (John 12:49,50; Luke 4:18-21)
   6. Spirit that makes no compromise with error (Matt. 16:6; 7:15)
   7. Spirit that condemns wickedness and hypocrisy. (Matt. 11:20-24; 23:13-36).
   8. Spirit "loves righteousness and hates iniquity" Hebrews 1:9 bears witness to the truth." (John 18:37); Testifies to the reward of righteousness and punishment of the wicked (Matt. 25:31-46) Weeps over the doomed (Luke 19:41-44).
   9. Christ was concerned about the lost and so should spiritual leaders. (Luke 15:3-7; Matt. 28:18-20).

VII. CARING LEADERSHIP WILL ESTABLISH PRIORITIES WITHIN THE BODY OF BELIEVERS.

A. People should take precedence over procedures; mission over methodology.

B. We make vision that sets goals–money, attendance and building. "When you catch up with your goals you are in trouble"–Robert Shuller.

C. We should exhibit a Christian attitude in all decisions:
1. Does the good of the church take precedence over personal whims?
2. Is talent of the membership more important than tradition?
3. Is flexibility in programming of more value than pontifical decisions?
4. Is servanthood viewed as the objective rather than domination?
5. Is there Christian conduct on the part of the leader which will enable him to influence others?

D. The bottom line is: WE NEED EACH OTHER AND ALL OF US NEED A MATURING RELATIONSHIP WITH JESUS CHRIST IF HE IS TO BE LORD OF OUR LIVES. "Be the kind of person you can live with, have principle to live by and have goals to live for."

VIII. THE RELATIONSHIP BETWEEN THE MINISTER AND THE ELDERSHIP IS VITAL TO THE HEALTH OF THE CONGREGATION.

During the 1970's & 80's there appeared to be a great deal of friction between the minister and the eldership among Christian Churches. There was competition between the two as to who was in charge. Many preachers during the period perceived the eldership as being the enemy to effective leadership. Non-cooperation between the two resulted in a stalemate that neutralized the leadership of both with the congregation experiencing no leadership The end result of the spirited competition was the firing of the preacher and sometimes a split in the congregation itself. In the twenty-first century many preachers have turned the table by minimizing the influence of the eldership and taking the lead in decision making. Scripturally, the preacher should be considered to be an elder among elders with a mutual concern for the church's well being. The preacher is called to the pulpit by the same congregation that elects the eldership. He is expected to be the visionary for leading the congregation and spearheading church growth. Some suggestions for the unity between the two parties are suggested as follows:

1. Maintain a friendly relationship regularly outside of scheduled business meetings.
2. Schedule social times in and outside of the church building.

3. Spend time in prayer preceding the business portion of the meeting.

4. Exchange information about needs of the members.

5. Entertain thoughts for consideration by all members of the group.

6. Avoid an up and down vote on motions on the floor and end with a consensus of the group.

7. Postpone controversial matters to allow time for all members to think about them.

8. Keep detailed records of discussed subjects for future discussions.

9. Avoid inconsequential matters that produce division.

10. Report the decisions of the group to the congregation routinely for clarification to all.

IX. WITHOUT RESPECT FOR LEADERS BY THOSE BEING LED, ANARCHY, CHAOS AND CONFUSION WILL RESULT WITH THE CHURCH BODY.

A. ONE OF THE THINGS TO GUARD AGAINST IS THE MATTER OF CHANGE:

A story that has circulated over the years was about a man whose sight left him. He sought the counsel of a trusted friend who prescribed a medicine for him. The man took the medicine regularly for four days and his sight returned to him, but he could no longer remember anything. His friend suggested a remedy for that, too. After a few days his memory came back to him, but he went blind again. This continued for some time after which the friend said to him, 'It looks like you will have to decide which you want–your sight or your memory.' The man thought for a moment and then said, 'I believe I would prefer my sight. I would rather see where I'm going than remember where I've been.' Fortunately we are not confronted with such a choice. We have the benefit of both. Leading is like driving a car. You have a rear view mirror to see what's behind you and a windshield to see what's in front of you. The difference is in the size of the mirror and the windshield. If you don't know something of the past it is difficult to map out the future. Memory and vision are complimentary, not opponents.

B. Changes in the church today: **COME TO THE AUCTION**. We need to be careful that we don't throw the baby out with the bath water. In adopting contemporary approach to leadership, worship and ministry we need to guard against eliminating essential Biblical truths and practices.

Over the years, someone gave me a definition of the Church that's worth sharing: "It is the fellowship of forgiven believers in Christ,

27

united by the Holy Spirit for the purpose of doing God's will for the glory of Christ Jesus".

C. TWO THINGS ARE IMPERATIVE FOR THE SURVIVAL OF THE LOCAL CHURCH AND TO MAINTAIN HER GROWTH:

1. The church must be founded upon Christ and the Word of Truth.
2. The leadership must be flexible in the area of Methodology.

The leadership must guard against Liberalism in Theology on the one hand and Legalism in Methodology on the other. . To depart from either could make the church ineffective or possibly spell the death of the local congregation.

The slogan of the Restoration Movement in the beginning was: "In matters of faith, unity; in matters of opinion, liberty; and in all things love." Our goal: "The restoration of primitive Christianity in its doctrine, its ordinances and its practice."

Throughout Jesus' ministry on earth, He was saying: Hear me! Follow me! Remember me! (1) "Bring them in". (2). "Build them up" (3) "Send them out".

D. THE MINISTER AND HIS STAFF

As the local church grows, the number of ministers on staff are needed to lead and equip the membership. Many churches have added Equippers as Secretaries, Youth, Education, Shepherding, Accounting, Building maintenance and Music and the list goes on. The late Dr. Leon Appel, then President of Lincoln Bible College, Lincoln, Illinois.,in an article entitled "THE MINISTER AND HIS STAFF", remembers that more than fifty years ago, there was no need for a church staff for the following reasons:

E. COMMUNICATION WITH THE CHURCH STAFF

"The heart of a multiple ministry is the happy relationship of those who work together in serving their people under the leadership of Christ."– *Wm. H. Leach* – HANDBOOK OF CHURCH MANAGEMENT.

The apostle Paul urges, "Encourage one another and build one another up."

An old adage says: "He who boosts another lifts himself." Lines of communication must be kept open between members of the staff.

A weekly staff meeting is advisable.

      1.   Communication is the road to understanding."

      2.   Probably the most difficult work the minister has to perform is to develop and maintain the spirit of harmony in a church staff, but it is also the most rewarding.

Churches have been hampered in the overall ministry and even split because of un-Christian relationships within the church staff. It is unforgivable for a staff member to draw a salary from the church and promote division at the same time.

These considerations will help the minister provide leadership for his staff so that the multiple ministry will be effective and the work coordinated.

X.   CHURCH LEADERS ARE PEOPLE MOTIVATORS.

Church members rarely can or will rise above the leadership. The present and the future of each congregation lies in the example set by the leaders which I have identified in acrostic form:

P romptness at meetings.
E fficiency in carrying out responsibilities.
O rderly procedures in meetings.
P reparedness in fulfilling responsibilities.
L oving in relationships with each other.
E ncourager of each other.

M annerly (Courteous).
O bjective in making decisions (Not self-centered).
T houghful of others (Considerate).
I nitiative in ministry. (Self-starter).
V isionary.
A mbitious (Set goals).
T rustworthy (Worthy of other's confidence).
O ptimistic (Positive attitude).
R eliable (Dependable).
S incere.

XI.   CHOOSING THE CHURCH STAFF.

    A.   "The members of the staff should be selected to fit the program of each church in such a way as to enable that church to render its maximum service." –Weldon Crossland.

      1.   Enlargement of the church staff should always begin in the area of greatest need.

2. Proper channels should be followed.
3. Outline a job description for each employee and let it be known what will be expected in inter-staff relationships.
   a. In theory, it is very easy to outline the tasks of a multiple ministry, but in practice it is very difficult.
   b. A growing church staff and program often necessitates a shifting of responsibilities from time to tine.
   c. Proper understanding of these things will avoid the "I wasn't hired to do that" syndrome.

XII. THE CONTINUING RELATIONSHIP IN A STAFF SITUATION.

(Leon Appel has set forth the following suggestions for which I concur from my own ministry.)

A. Avoid the occupational hazards faced in Christian work.
   1. Jealousy of another's success, praise, prominence or salary.
   2. Sensitiveness, which cherishes hurts and nourishes grudges.
   3. Criticisms
   4. Selfishness which says, "My work must have the right of way."
   5. Disloyalty to the total program, to the minister or the decisions of the group. .

XIII. PORTRAIT OF A LEADER. (Acts 20:17-32).

A. LEADERS ARE CARING SERVANTS .

B. LEADERS ARE MOTIVATORS. Finally, He says, "I have showed you all things, how that so labouring ye ought to support the weak and to remember the words of the Lord Jesus, how he said, 'It is more blessed to give than to receive.'" (20:35)

C. LEADERS ARE STANDARD BEARERS (MODELS).

> Isn't it strange that Princes and Kings
> And clowns that caper in sawdust rings;
> And common folks like you and me
> Are builders of eternity.
> To each is given a bag of tools,
> A shapeless mass and a book of rules;
> And each must fashion 'ere life is flown
> A stumbling block or a stepping stone.

Chapter 4

THE CHURCH POSITIONED FOR GROWTH

"Now therefore ye are no more strangers and foreigners, but fellow citizens with the saints, and of the household of God; And are built upon the foundation of the apostles and prophets, Jesus Christ himself being the chief corner stone. In whom all the building fitly framed together growth unto the holy temple in the Lord: In whom ye also are builded together for an habitation of God through the Spirit." –Ephesians 2:19-22.

The obvious lesson we learn from the Scriptures is that the church consists of redeemed people, not the building. Growth refers not only to numbers but spiritual development of the members as well. However, the growth of the church from the beginning is recorded by Luke, in Acts 2:41, when about 3,000 responded to the message of Peter and were baptized. Luke updates the number to 5,000 responses to the gospel in Acts 4:4.

Following the persecution of the church in Jerusalem with the martyrdom of Stephen, the church scattered abroad, except the apostles, and went everywhere preaching the word. (Acts. 8:4).

The church either grows or stagnates. The last words of Jesus to the apostles prior to his ascension were what we have come to know as the Great Commission. "Go ye therefore, and teach all nations, baptizing them in the name of the Father, and of the Son, and of the Holy Ghost: Teaching them to observe all things whatsoever I have commanded you: and, lo, I am with you always, even unto the end of the world." (Matthew 28:19,20) (KJV).

Many people today tend to shy away from a large congregation,

31

preferring a small group fellowship. My question through the years to this mentality has been: "At what point would you want the cut-off number to be, after you join or before?" Back in the 1970's the Bethany Christian Church in Anderson, Indiana experienced an explosive growth in numbers. We had reached the mega-church category before the increase among Christian churches and Churches of Christ took place. . Our membership soared to 1700. My purpose in this chapter is to relate some of the growth principles that worked for us. The first premise must be the recognition that growth is the purpose for which the church exists. When the church does not grow it cannot be pleasing to God. "Herein is my Father glorified, that ye bear much fruit, so shall ye be my disciples" (John 15:8). Fruit bearing is the end purpose of the tree and Christians are the end purpose of the church.

For the congregation to grow in numbers, believers must be equipped for leadership and ministry. Paul outlines this procedure in Ephesians 4:11-16. The problems of churches with declining membership stems from the following:

1. A lack of faith on the part of the leaders.
2. A lack of faithfulness on the part of the membership.

The church of the 1st Century grew by leaps and bounds. The growth of the church in today's world can profit by discovering the nature of that body of believers and the source of growth.

1. The New Testament Church was never a place, but always a people.
2. The New Testament Church was never a Saviour, but always the saved.
3. The New Testament Church did not count numbers, but made numbers count.

I.   THE NEW TESTAMENT CHURCH WAS A PREACHING CHURCH.

A.   We have already noted that the preaching of Peter on Pentecost resulted in 3,000 responding to the invitation with continued responses to their witnessing.

B.   Paul declared that the preaching of the cross was the power of God to all who believed. (1 Cor. 1:18-21).

C.   Paul urged Timothy to preach the word in season and out of season. (2 Timothy 4:2-4).

II.   THE NEW TESTAMENT CHURCH WAS A LOVING CHURCH.

A.   Jesus said the first and greatest commandment was to love God

32

and the second to love one's neighbor as oneself (Matt. 22:36-40).

B. "This is my commandment, that ye love one another, as I have loved you." (John 15:12).

C. "If we love one another, God dwelleth in us, and His love is perfected in us. (1 John 4:12b).

D. "And walk in love, as Christ also hath loved us..." (Eph. 5:2).

E. Edwin Markum has best described the loving relationship that should prevail on the part of believers:

> "He drew a circle and shut me out;
> Rebel, heretic, a thing to flout.
> But love and I had a wit to win,
> We drew a circle that took him in."

F. Paul best describes what love is in I Corinthians Chapter 13.

III. THE NEW TESTAMENT CHURCH WAS A MINISTERING CHURCH.

A. The Jerusalem church shared their possessions with each other (Acts 4:32).

B. When problems developed with neglected widows in the church, the problem was met with the appointment of Deacons to take care of the problem. (Acts. 6:1-7).

C. Jesus equated our ministry to others in need to our ministry to Him. (Matthew25:31-46).

D. James defines pure religion as ministering to the fatherless and the widows (James 1:27) and contends that faith without works is dead (James 2:14-17).

E. A live church is one that is sensitive to the needs of people everywhere–inmates in prison, sick in the hospital, aging in nursing homes and the poverty stricken.

IV. THE NEW TESTAMENT CHURCH WAS A SHARING CHURCH.

A. It was no accident that Luke records that the disciples were called Christians first at Antioch." (Acts. 11:26).

1. It was at Antioch that the gospel was preached to the Grecians as well as the Jews and many believed. (Acts 11:19-21).

33

2. Upon hearing that the Jerusalem church was facing a famine, they determined to receive an offering and sent it to the brethren there. (Acts. 11:27-29).

V. THE NEW TESTAMENT CHURCH WAS A REACHING CHURCH (MISSIONARY MINDED)

A. The followers of Christ reached out by sharing the gospel under threat of persecution. (Acts 8:1).

B. At Antioch the brethren desired to get the Word out and set apart Paul and Barnabas for a missionary journey to share the gospel. (Acts 13:2,3). These acts of outreach were sufficient for them to be identified as "Christians."

VI. THE NEW TESTAMENT CHURCH WAS A CARING CHURCH.

A. The church in Galatia gave heed to Paul's exhortation: "Bear ye one another's burdens and so fulfill the law of Christ." (Galatians 6:2).

B. Paul admonished the Corinthians to be united in their testimony, attitude, judgment and pattern of life. (1 Cor. 1:10-13).

C. Jesus' personal prayer was for the unity of all believers (John 17).

D. They cared for Christ the head of the church and for one another.

VII. THE LOCAL CHURCH CAN COME ALIVE AND GROW BY IMITATING THEIR EXAMPLE.

A. Local churches are like people; they have their own personalities. They will develop a personality that reflects both the leadership and membership, both the members' concerns and commitments.

B. When the church is alive and reaching out to the community, it will grow in numbers as well as influence.

VIII. THE CHURCH WILL GROW . . .

A. Where the Word is **preached** in love from the pulpit. Preaching is primary, not secondary. The Word of God will "disturb the comforted and comfort the disturbed." (Hebrews 4:12; Isaiah 55:10-11.)

B. Where the Word is **taught** in the classroom. Methods will and should vary, but the textbook must always be the primary tool, not secondary. (2 Timothy 3:14-17).

C. Where the Word is **put into practice** by the membership–Most people would rather see a sermon than hear one any day. (1 Peter 5:3).

D. Where the Word is **shared in** rap sessions, home Bible studies, prayer breakfasts, social gatherings, over the back fence with neighbors, etc.

E. Where the Lord's PLAN and PURPOSE for His church is followed.

    1. There must be a **dedicated leadership**---The preacher is the coach–He sets the mood for the church–He should be visionary, optimistic, enthusiastic, passionate, longsuffering, confident, humble, energetic and non-discriminating.

Elders and deacons should be scripturally and spiritually qualified. They should desire the office of service (1 Timothy 3:1). Their talents and abilities should be suited to the position for which they are chosen. (Eph. 4:11)

They should be spiritual men whom the congregation hold in confidence and with respect. There is no place for either a Slanderer or a Flatterer. The first is one who says behind your back what he wouldn't say to your face while the second is one who says things to your face he wouldn't say behind your back.

PLEASE, GOD, GIVE US MEN!

Give us men with eyes to see
– Visions as they ought to be;
Men who champion the right,
Men with courage to smite;
men with boldness to begin,
Men who dare to fight and win;
Men who will not stoop to wrong,
or to please the lauding throng;
Men who'd perish with the just
Ere' they'd violate their trust;
Who the hosts of sin defy,
Holding Christ's own banner high!

    2. There must be an **activated membership.**

The church and its ministry is something that people ought to be able to get excited about. We have to destroy the myth of separation of clergy and laity which we condemn, but often practice.

The congregation must draw the people. As the members share their enthusiasm with the church and invite their friends and neighbors, they will come to the services and activities. Statistics prove this.

*The babes in Christ must be fed and given spiritual direction to guide them through successive stages of growth: Dependence, Independence and Interdependence.

*The membership must be educated and trained to use their God-given talents for the Lord. The word used for EQUIPPED in Ephesians 4:12 is *katartismon* from the verb *katartizein*. It is used also in the New Testament for disciplining an offender until he is fit to take his place again within the fellowship of the church (Galatians 6:1).

3. There must be an **activated fellowship**.

Koinonia is the Greek word for the New Testament Fellowship in the 1st century and indicates a sharing and blending of lives which produces harmony and well-being.

*In a fellowship of Christians where the Holy Spirit can freely work, cliques and quarreling factions cannot develop. We are faced with an identity crisis in our world today and this often carries over into the church. People want to feel that they are known, wanted and needed by others. Jesus showed this kind of concern in His encounter with Zacchaeus. (:Luke 19:1-10). "Zacchaeus:" "He knows my name"; "Make haste and come down from there" "He wants me."; "for today I must abide at thy house." "He needs me."

*John says, "If we say we have fellowship with Him and walk in darkness, we lie and do not the truth; but if we walk in the light as He is in the light we have fellowship one with another and the blood of Jesus Christ, His Son, cleanseth us from all sin." (1 John 1:6).

IX. THE CHURCH WILL COME ALIVE AND GROW THROUGH A DEDICATED LEADERSHIP.

A. A good administrator will:

1. Delegate responsibility.
2. Build confidence in his ideas and programs by not acting too hastily; by attempting change slowly and by presenting well-planned, workable ideas.
3. Be quick to give credit to others for accomplishments. Much can be accomplished if one is not particular about who gets the credit.
4. Follow through on projects. It is not how many things you start, but what you finish that counts.

5. Outline clearly your goals and programs and keep them before the people.
6. Provide leadership training for areas of responsibility and service.
7. Expect faithfulness in fulfilling responsibilities and demonstrate this characteristic in one's own work.

B. The Do's in Effective Administration:
1. Visualize the working church.
2. Organize your program.
3. Deputize your workers.
4. Departmentalize your areas of service and leadership.
5. Vitalize the entire program by allowing the Holy Spirit to lead in new fields of endeavor.
6. Supervise the workers.
7. Publicize the total program.

C. The Don'ts in Effective Administration.
1. Don't delegate authority to one person. Avoid creating a situation where too much authority is vested in one person. Even the preacher should not assume authority to make major decisions without sharing first with the eldership and staff members.
2. Don't criticize the elders and deacons publicly or attempt to bypass them in decision-making when in disagreement.
3. Don't purposely try to antagonize the opposition; make friends of them.
4. Don't compromise your convictions on matters of faith.
5. Don't try to change ineffective methods of procedure over night.
6. Don't over-react to criticism. Constructive criticism should be embraced.

X. WHERE THERE IS VISION AND ADEQUATE LONG-RANGE PLANNING.

A. Long range planning is important for goals to motivate the congregation. (For a major project, 5 to 10 years may be needed).
1. A church that meets today's needs tomorrow is always behind.
2. Planning for the future should include building expansion for both worship and education, parking facilities, personnel as well as goals in evangelism, missions and benevolence, church planting and recruiting young people for specialized Christian service.

B. Provide adequate facilities for babies, children and youth but don't neglect the elderly. Graded worship and Educational programs are important to attract young couples.

C. There should be flexibility in methods and programming to meet the changing needs.

D. Proper division of leadership into functioning committees or ministry teams is a must to fulfill the ministry of the church. Include departments of Evangelism, Missions, Shepherding, Youth, Worship, Education, Properties, Finance and Stewardship, Plus Staff as the congregation grows.

E. Establish stewardship goals that include tithing challenges for the members. Plan financial stability for future building expansion.

XI. ESTABLISHING PRIORITIES WITHIN THE BODY OF CHRIST.

A. Richard DeVos, dynamic president of Amway, relates in his book BELIEVE some rare insight into the rise and fall of various institutions including the local church. If the church is not careful she will inevitably and gradually follow the four-stage changes: (1) the creating stage; (2) the organizing stage; (3)the defending stage; (4) the stage of "dividing the spoils."

The first stage begins with a dream, a time of building when the energies of all the people are constantly poured into a united effort to evangelize and build up the body of Christ. This is why so many new congregations grow so rapidly during their initial enthusiasm.

The second stage is the time of growth and progress when the members divert time and energy from the building and creating function and devote it to organizing and managing what has been created. It is necessary and important work but unfortunately the managerial work is usually done by the people who formerly were on the front end of the group, the building end.

With the group busy managing what has already been developed, the work of evangelism is sub-contracted – usually to paid staff members.

The third stage is the time when the primary concern becomes that of holding the line and defending the acquisitions of the group from outside competition or encroachment. The congregation becomes obsessed with maintaining the "status quo" with little thought of growth or expansion of the ministries. Energies are spent in just "feeding the flock" and working to hold the young people.

The fourth stage consists too frequently of the managerial groups turning their energies inward and members fighting among themselves to divide the spoils. They forget what it was like to be out there on the cutting edge, sacrificing to create and build from nothing. They assume that new converts will continue to be made, operating expenses will always be met, and a power struggle begins for position and recognition. As excitement and mission is lost, stagnation sets in, growth stops and downward momentum begins and accelerates.

What is the answer to the downward spiral? GO BACK TO STAGE ONE!

The ministry is often carried out within the church body within a hostile environment. The following may be helpful in building attitudes that are positive in such a negative environment.

Author Kent M. Keith was a sophomore at Harvard University in the 1960's when he first wrote "The Paradoxical Commandments," a manifesto about doing good in a crazy, ungrateful world. Since his Harvard days, Keith's commandments have taken on a life of their own. They have been quoted by the Boy Scouts of America and written on inspirational office memos, classroom handouts and internet sites around the world. They were quoted, circulated and appropriated by countless people around the world and back again. They even served as a source of inspiration for Mother Teresa who hung these commandments on the wall of her children's home in Calcutta. They are as follows:

1. People are illogical, unreasonable, and self-centered. **Love them anyway.**
2. If you do good, people will accuse you of selfish ulterior motives. **Do good anyway**
3. If you are successful, you will win false friends and true enemies. **Succeed anyway**.
4. The good you do today will be forgotten tomorrow. **Do good anyway.**

5. Honesty and frankness make you vulnerable. **Be honest and frank anyway**.
6. The biggest men and women with the biggest ideas can be shot down by the smallest men and women with the smallest minds. **Think big anyway.**
7. People favor underdogs but follow only top dogs. **Fight for a few underdogs anyway.**
8. What you spend years building may be destroyed overnight. **Build anyway.**
9. People really need help but may attack you if you do help them. **Help people anyway.**

10. Give the world the best you have and you'll get kicked in the teeth. **Give the world the best you have anyway**.

The bottom line of leadership is WE LEAD MOST BY EXAMPLE! WE CANNOT TEACH WHAT WE DO NOT KNOW & WE CANNOT LEAD WHERE WE ARE UNWILLING TO GO.

In challenging members of our congregation to minister, it is important that we point out the difference between a JOB and a MINISTRY.

*Some people have a JOB in the church: others involve themselves in a MINISTRY. What's the difference? If you are doing it just because no one else will, it's a JOB. If you are doing it to serve the Lord, it's a MINISTRY.

*If you quit because someone criticizes you, it's a JOB. If you keep on serving, it's a MINISTRY.

*If you'll do it only so long as it does not interfere with your other activities, It's a JOB. If you're committed to staying with it even when it means letting go of other things, it's a MINISTRY.

*If you quit because no one praises you, or thanks you, it's a JOB. If you stay with it even though no one recognizes your efforts, it's a MINISTRY.

*It's hard to get excited about a JOB. It's almost impossible not to be excited about a MINISTRY.

*If our concern is success, it's a JOB. If our concern is faithfulness, it's a MINISTRY An average church is filled with people doing JOBS. A great and growing church is filled with people involved in MINISTRY. Where do you fit in? What about our church?

*If God calls you to a MINISTRY, don't treat it like a JOB. If you have a JOB in the church, give it up and find a MINISTRY. God doesn't want us feeling stuck with a JOB, but excited and faithful to HIM in a MINISTRY.

A THOUGHT TO PONDER!

Which kind are you?

A lot of Christians are like wheelbarrows – not good unless pushed.
Some are like canoes–they need to be paddled.
Some are like kites-if you don't keep a string on them, they fly away.
Some are like kittens–they are more contented when petted.
Some are like a football–you can't tell what way they will bounce next.
Some are like balloons–full of wind and ready to blow up.
Some are like trailers–they have to be pulled.
Some are like lights–they keep going on and off.

And there are those who always seek to let the Holy Spirit lead them.

REASONS FOR LIFE

I don't know how to say it, but somehow it seems to me,
That maybe we are stationed where God wants us to be.
That the little place I'm filling is the reason for my birth
And just to do the work I do, He sent me down to earth.
If God had wanted otherwise, I reckon He'd have made
Me just a little different, of a worse or better grade.
And since God knows and understands all things of
Land and sea, I fancy that He placed me here,
Just where He wanted me to be.
Sometimes I get to thinking, as my labors I review,
That I should like a higher place with greater things to do.
But I come to the conclusion, when the envying is stilled,
That the post to which God sent me is the post He wanted filled.
So, I plod along and struggle in the hope, when day is through,
That I'm really necessary to things God wants to do.
And there isn't any service I can give, which I should scorn,
For it may be just the reason God allowed that I be born
–Author Unknown

Edward Smith, Minister a few years ago at the English Christian Church in Carrollton, Ky. wrote a column on Church Growth that is still relevant for the church to grow in the twenty-first century.

"Growth is the purpose for which the church exists" He refers to the Laws of Growth Applied previously presented by A Flake back in 1920.

The principles of growth are: (1) Enrollment increases in proportion to the number of workers to students, reaching a maximum at the ratio of ten students to one worker. (2) Sunday school classes reach their maximum growth in a few months after their beginning. (3) New units grow faster, win more to Christ, provide more workers and tend to stimulate a higher quality of work than existing units. (4) Age group grading has proved to be the most functional way of starting new units. (5) Promotion recognizes the natural laws of growth and development. (6) Enrollment and attendance increase in proportion to the number of personal, quality visits. (7). The church building sets the pattern for the shape and size of the Bible school. (8) Reaching the lost depends upon proper delegation of responsibility of a particular Sunday school unit. (9) Effective reaching of prospects depends upon the consistent use of each principle of growth. Simply applying one or two principles does not mean so much growth will occur. They simply allow the church to grow."

In my 29-year ministry at Anderson, Indiana the numerical growth came about through many different outreach procedures:

1. We advertized through the local News papers about our church.

2. We scheduled many well-known preachers and singing groups to the services regularly.

3. We kept the congregation and prospects informed through the church paper: "The Bethany Christian."

4. We maintained a file of "prospects" of individuals and families with no removals until mission was accomplished.

5. We projected messages to the community by an attractive outside bulletin board that was maintained on a weekly basis.

6. I maintained a personal relationship with the Religious Editor of the local newspaper that provided even front page publicity during our building expansions and special days.

7. We made plans and executed building expansion promptly as needed–Worship Center, Educational Building and Family Life Center.

8. The parking lot was expanded to provide adequate parking.

9. The acreage on which our buildings stood, across from the local Highland High School, was donated by a generous member. Prior to starting our first church plant, a generous member left his entire estate to the church.

10. We increased our giving to Missions annually and recruited forty-two young people for Bible Colleges to prepare for full-time Christian Service. That number has increased even more in recent years.

11. We maintained an organized calling program of individuals in homes throughout our community.

12. The leadership planned and executed efforts to plant other Christian Churches in Anderson and surrounding communities.

13. We practiced the "Equipping Ministry" for the outreach and ongoing function of the church.

14. We encouraged the members to reach out to their neighbors and friends and bring them in.

15. We resisted separatism from the religious community but rather reached out and fellowshipped with other congregations for special days.

16. We conducted annual stewardship seminars to encourage our members to try tithing.

17. Our leadership initiated a Summer Internship Program of bringing one and sometimes more than one Bible College student each Summer for hands-on experience before they graduated from College.

18. The congregation was blessed with many generous special financial gifts for the Lord's work through the years.

BROKEN FOR A BLESSING

In order to keep the building up for current needs, remodeling is required to maintain proper standards. Remodeling is a way of transforming and updating a building to make it more appealing, efficient or useful. Usually, it involves a redesign on the inside of the building, but it can also include the outside of the property.

Those who have been through the process of remodeling know how extensive and upsetting it can be. Even in the best of circumstances, workers will still create dust and chaos. Yet, in order to enjoy something old being made new, you have to go through the process of remodeling. The same is true when you view God's plan for your life.

There are times in the life of every believer when he or she will go through a time of remodeling. It is a time when God is updating our lives by stripping away old thoughts and habits and replacing them with His truths and principles. Instead of calling it remodeling, we call the process "brokenness."

Just like the beginning phases of a construction program, the outcome may be hard to imagine especially when things have been torn apart. Sheetrock is missing and tools are scattered from one end of your building to the other. However, before we can do the same, we have to be willing to allow God to give us spiritual eyes to see life from His perspective. After all, He is the One who holds the blueprints to our lives. Paul knew that there were many glorious benefits to the times he faced suffering. The greatest was his testimony of faith in Jesus Christ. No matter what befell him, Paul continued to trust in the One who had saved him and was in charge of his life. Have you come to a time of brokenness? If so, let God remodel your life, and you will be amazed at the outcome.

Life seems to be out of our control. .At times God allows these situations because He knows they will move us closer to Him, and when we get closer to Him we will discover that He is more than we ever imagined Him to be.

*Church growth can result in pressures we never dreamed of. Unless bathed in prayer, tensions can result within leadership that can test the church's determination to address problems and move ahead. . Dealing with church leadership conflicts and individual discouragement will be addressed in another chapter of this discourse.

Chapter 5

FALTERS AT THE ALTAR AND OTHER BLOOPERS

It would be well to begin by defining ALTAR. I have chosen to use this word for the sake of convenience and rhyme. The word Altar was a word used again and again in the Old Testament by Noah, Abraham, Moses, Joshua and others. The Hebrew word for altar means "a place of slaughter or sacrifice." It was the central place in the worship of the Israelites. The golden altar of incense (Exodus 30:1-10) stood just before the veil inside the tabernacle that separated the most holy place from the rest of the worship area.

Priests burned incense on this altar every day so its fragrance would fill the tabernacle.

The house of worship in the New Dispensation does not need such an altar.

Elisha A. Hoffman carries this theme in the lyrics of his Hymn, "Is Your All on the Altar?" The chorus reads: "Is your all on the altar of sacrifice laid? Your heart, does the Spirit control? You can only be blest and have peace and sweet rest, As you yield Him your body and soul." Through the years Christians have had difficulty of properly identifying the different areas of our houses of worship. Figuratively speaking, I suppose each of us are called upon to place our lives on the altar of commitment to the Lord.

As to the worship center itself, Christians have had difficulty in properly identifying the different areas of the church building.

At Butler University, School of Religion, I chose to do a paper on "The Externals of Christian Worship." In my research I discovered that the

Architectural designations of the building were as follows: NARTHEX–The Entryway; NAVE–The main seating area of the worshipers; The CHANCEL–The elevated area of the pulpit, choir, and leaders in worship.

My desire in this Chapter is to share some areas that were humorous but also problematic in carrying out my ministry. Stay with me as we share some of these experiences.

My very first funeral, was in the Summer following my second year at Johnson Bible College I was asked to do the funeral for a neighbor who happened to be a self-styled Atheist. That posed a real problem in reading the obituary. It actually helped me establish priorities in memorial services for the deceased throughout my ministry. I made the obituary one segment of the address but concentrated on a message for the living .Funerals have, through the years, offered an opportunity to set forth the importance of a persons' serious relationship with Christ. Early on, I adopted the words of an unknown author and made them the opening statement at most every funeral message that I delivered. The words are as follows:

"One sweetly, solemn thought comes to me O'er and O'er;
I'm nearer home today than I've ever been before.
Nearer my Father's house where the many mansions be;
Nearer the great white Throne, near the crystal sea.
Nearer the bound of life where we lay life's burdens down;
Nearer leaving the cross; Nearer gaining the crown;
But lying somewhere between is an unknown stream,
That leads at last to life.
Father, be near as my feet slip o'er the brink;
It may be that I'm nearer home,
Nearer now than I think."

When I made it known that I was going to study to be a preacher, my Aunt Ruby Compton, who was very opinionated on most subjects, challenged my plans to be a preacher. She indicated that preachers are targets for criticism and are extremely underpaid. But, she declared, if you're intent upon being one, why not be a Methodist preacher since they were assigned to the church by a Bishop. My response was simply that I should be able to hold a pulpit by my preparation and delivery without being appointed to a church by a superior.

My choice was later confirmed by her when I returned to my home church to deliver the sermon. Among my supporters present were her and Cousin Alice. At the invitation both came forward to be immersed. The baptism took place in the Ohio river at Brookport, Illinois where most baptisms were held. When we waded into the deep water for the baptism, though I had been baptized in the same river and had witnessed many being put under the water, it never occurred to me that there was a wrong way verses a right way to conduct the baptism. Rather than put her under the water with head upstream, enabling the current to lift her up on her feet coming out of the water, I did it the other way around so upon coming up out of the water the current began to carry her downstream. Needless to say, I almost lost her. Through the years she contended that I tried to drown her. I soon learned the old adage: "Experience is a hard teacher; she gives her tests first and her lessons afterwards."

Speaking of baptisms, the story was circulated about a congregation whose members were battling over the use of the piano in worship. On a given Sunday, the piano was utilized for the song service. Then, the congregation would arrive to discover the piano missing, leaving the congregation to worship a cappella. After several alternating experiences the piano was missing on a permanent basis. According to the account, three years passed with no one having uncovered the mystery. Then one Sunday there was a response to the invitation and when preparation was made for the baptism, they discovered the missing piano in the baptistery. It spoke volumes about the outreach of the congregation.

During my ministry at the Normanda Christian Church, Tipton, Indiana, we were conducting a great revival at the church with a large number of responses to the Invitation. Among them was a millionaire whom nobody had been able to reach. He was instructed to change his street clothes into a baptismal robe along with the others. Much to my surprise and that of the congregation, he appeared at the baptistery dressed only in his long-handled underwear. This brought some snickers from the shocked audience. He was happy over his decision and wanted to show his appreciation and financial support for the revival and demonstrated it later by pressing a quarter in my hand to help the cause.

At Bethany Christian Church baptisms were held on a regular basis and sometimes during all three services. At one particular service a young ten year old girl dressed for her baptism but was obviously frightened to go through with it. She was not quite sure she wanted to be put under the water and began fighting the procedure. We struggled for several minutes with water splashing in every direction while the congregation looked on anxiously; after which she broke away from my grasp and ran out of the baptistry to the dressing room. As far as I know, she never again made the decision of be baptized and that was the only candidate for baptism that I did not unsuccessfully accomplish throughout my sixty-four years of ministry.

Preachers are notorious, I'm told, for speeding. I was most fortunate in that department until I was stopped for deservedly speeding three times in one month. On one of these, I was returning from a preaching trip that had taken me away from family for some time and was in a hurry to get back to Anderson from the Indianapolis International Airport. I was driving on cruise and exceeded the speed limit through Ingalls, Indiana. I was stopped by a Highway Patrolman who asked for my drivers' license. As I proceeded to hand him my license, he said, "I don't really need that. I know who you are." Surprised, I responded. "I don't think I know who you are, Sir. Who am I? To which he responded without hesitation: "You're my PREACHER." He continued the exchange by giving me a warning ticket and a lecture on safe driving. As I pondered the incident I wondered why I did not know him. It so happened that his mother belonged to the Bethany Church and he had attended Sunday School as a child. He had grown up and moved away so I did not recognize him.

In my five year ministry at Mt. Vernon, Ky. I learned a lot about how to deal with alcoholics. I had a number of counseling sessions with the brother-in-law of our church organist. It was only when he was over the top in his alcoholic binges that he would show up at the parsonage asking to speak to me. My wife, Kathryn, was fed up with his visits and informed him to come back when he was sober if he wanted to talk to the preacher. On one occasion he wanted me to drive him out in the country to see his ex-wife and children at their mother's place. I agreed on the condition that he be sober. On the way there, he pulled out his bottle that was hidden in a paper bag. I threatened to turn around, but he promised good behavior. Upon arrival, he argued with his former mate in the middle of the road. I was an unhappy camper, to say the least. Loading him in the car, I drove him back to within a mile of town and made him exit and walk the rest of the way back. He continued to be, among others, an ongoing challenge to my early ministry.

While serving the Shepherdsville Christian Church in Kentucky for a short time, performed a wedding for two couples; whereupon the clerk's office called me in to inform me that the marriages were not valid because I had not registered and was not properly bonded to perform marriages. To become eligible I had to have two of my elders to sign for me. Each state has its own policies for performing marriage ceremonies.

The Summer of 1947 that I spent in Shepherdsville, Kentucky, I had no transportation to carry on the work of the church, so Miss Mattie Bailey, a member of the church, loaned me her Model A Ford to drive. Many things were broken on the car including the brakes and the front passenger seat. I volunteered to pick up the Baptist and Methodist Minister s on the way to a Preacher 's meeting. The Baptist sat in the back, and the Methodist chose to sit up front in the passenger seat. I forgot to warn him that the seat was not fasted down to the floor, so when I took off with a lurch, the seat in which je was sitting folded and he ended up in the lap of the Baptist preache r. It was a most embarrassing moment.

In 1948, after I graduated from College, I and my new bride, Kathryn Turnbull, moved to Mt. Vernon, Ky., to serve the church there. The first slip-up in accepting Kentucky hospitality was in connection with an invitation to dinner at the Luther Peytons. We had hardly finished the meal when it dawned upon me t hat we had been invited to the Coffey house the same evening. I proceeded to kick my wife under the table and make an excuse that we had to take care of some emergency. When we arrived at the Coffey's they were patiently waiting our arrival with a table laden with delicious food. We pretended to be hungry and proceeded to indulge, even though we were already stuffed from the meal we had just eaten. I began to keep a date book after that debacle to prevent it from happening again.

After settling in the new parsonage the leadership provided for us, I was asked by the Principal of the local High School to teach a typing class, plus a night class for adults. With pay for these classes and my salary of $25 a week, we purchased a brand new Dodge vehicle. We had hardly broken in when the Peytons asked us to take them to Hazard, Kentucky to see their son and family. This was a hurried trip requiring us a quick return the same evening for a wedding rehearsal. On the way, because of hairpin curves and heavy rainfall, we had a head-on collision with a pick-up truck. Then we were hit from behind by another vehicle. The car was totaled, and Kathryn, sleeping in the front seat at the time, received a concussion. We were transported to a Clinic in Hyden where I was carried up 24 flights of steps and my wife walked up. After emergency treatment, it was decided that she needed further treatment in a Hazard hospital, where we spent three days where she was under treatment and observation and I stood by in my blood soaked clothes. She constantly called for her father while not recognizing that I was her husband.

The Mt. Vernon Funeral home volunteered their ambulance to transport us back to our home where Kathryn spent three weeks bedridden in a world of her own.

In our ministry at Carlisle, Kentucky, I taught the adult Broadcasters class on Sunday morning. For three of the years at Christmas, I received a special gift. The first year they presented me with a new Bible. The 2nd year I received some beautiful luggage. The third year they presented me with four new tires for my vehicle. I was never sure whether there was a hidden farewell in the three gestures. One day I stopped at the church, parked my vehicle temporarily on the steep street across from the church with the brakes on for safety. Snow and ice covered the streets. About fifteen minutes inside, I returned to find my car missing. I then noticed a large crowd had gathered at the foot of the hill. Upon further investigation I discovered that it was my vehicle that had slid down the hill on its own and jumped the curb, and the front end rested on the front porch of the town chiropractor causing no damage to his house nor my car.

While at the Bethany Christian Church in Anderson, there were a number of bloopers, but the most outstanding one happened following the remodeling of the church sanctuary. I had heard about the Southland Christian Church in Lexington, Kentucky conducting a sin burning service. Taking a cue from Wayne Smith, I planned one in our building. The preparation was ill advised with a large candle placed in the middle of a large serving tray that rested in turn on a flower stand. We had an inspiring musical concert by a renowned singer from Indianapolis. Every person was given a piece of paper and a pencil for them to write a sin in their life they wanted to be ridden of by placing it over the candle of the burning service. As the papers were placed on the candle, the buildup created a fire that was soon out of hand. Without warning the tray holding the candle toppled to the floor of the newly laid carpet. Fortunately, the local fire marshal, who was a member of the church, and present at the service, rushed forward and put out the fire. I was later informed by him that the next time I planned to even light a candle in the church to alert him ahead of time so he could have the fire truck parked in the parking lot. Fortunately, I survived being fired by the elders.

On another occasion at Bethany, in the middle of a Sunday evening service, one of the deacons came quietly to the pulpit and handed me a note, instructing me that the alarms had been sounding in the city of an impending tornado for the area. I was to quickly but quietly dismiss the people and instruct them to proceed downstairs to the storm room. I ignored the note and finished the sermon and pronounced the benediction. By that time the danger had passed, but I was lectured by the local firemen and ambulance driver for my deliberate ignoring of the note.

At another evening service during a long-lasting drought when the farmers' crops were drying up, a hard rain moved in to our city. One of our elders, who was a wealthy farmer, was so thankful for the rain that he told me after the service that he had put in a $100 bill in the offering plate to show his thankfulness of the good rain. Arriving home, a few miles north of the church, I received a phone call from him. saying that it had not rained a drop of rain at his place and he wanted his $100 bill back.

I was asked to perform a marriage in Cincinnati, Ohio for my wife's nephew and his fiancé, graduates of Milligan College. The state only permits ministers of Ohio Churches to be eligible. Therefore, the Minister of the church was called upon to sign the license and make the marriage legal. In the state of Indiana most any person performing the ceremony is eligible to perform weddings. For this particular wedding, I was an hour late for the rehearsal the night before due to crossing the time line between Indiana and Ohio.

In my 64 years of Ministry I tied the knot for 555 couples and had equal number of funerals. Needless to say, there were some very memorable experiences in both categories. Space allow me to only reflect upon only a few of these.

In Mt. Vernon, Kentucky, before pre-marital counseling was mandated in my ministry, I was awakened one night at midnight by twin brothers who urgently wanted to marry twin sisters in a double wedding ceremony. I finally consented, and we performed the simple ceremony in a frigid church sanctuary. Standing over the large cold air intake register, one groom dropped the ring, intended for his bride, down the register. The ceremony was completed, and later we retrieve the ring. They did have their licenses to make it legal.

Throughout the twenty-nine years at the Bethany Christian Church, there were many falters during the ceremonies. Some of these included a bridesmaid's fainting during the ceremony and rescued from a fall by the father of the bride. In another situation, the florist messed up on the time of the wedding, and the disappointed bride delayed the wedding and hour until the florist scrambled to put the bouquets together and have them delivered across town. In another situation I forgot the name of the groom and substituted a different one. The couple never forgave me for the blunder .At the wedding of our church organist I forgot to allow the groom to kiss the bride at the close of the ceremony. Not to be outdone, they stopped at the end of the aisle, embraced and engaged in a passionate kiss while the audience cheered wildly.

It is always possible that anything can go wrong with the best of planning. However, there was one wedding that tops all miscues. It went something like this: At a counseling session before the wedding, the couple gave me their license, as required by me in advance of the wedding day. . Upon examination I discovered that it was a blank. The bride to be, it seemed, was a friend to the girl in the Clerk's office and she delivered the license to her later but picked up a blank instead of the proper one. . That should have been a warning that things were not going to go well. On the day of the wedding, a guest singer passed out during her song and a group of men from her church gathered around her praying. I was watching from behind the choir loft. I exited and approached the men by saying, "Gentlemen, I also believe in prayer but I think in this situation, what she needs is air"! She revived and sang two other songs. In the meantime, it was time to begin the wedding, whereupon the groom explained that his best man had not arrived. After thirty minutes delay, he arrived breathlessly with a flimsy excuse. Confident, finally, we proceeded to begin when the groom suddenly realized that he had left the rings back in his home. We scrambled around to find replacements among us. The ceremony seemed to come off without a hitch until the end when the couple lit the unity candle with their individual candles. At that point the bride's veil caught fire and the groom came to the rescue to extinguish the blaze. The whole ordeal reminded me of the message on a plane being flown by automatic pilot. The passengers, after being told over the speaker that everything was fine heard the follow-up assurance:: "Be assured that nothing can go wrong, go wrong, go wrong." My experiences with weddings taught me otherwise.

The gratuitous fee for wedding performances varied over time. In the early days of the sixties the voluntary gift was usually $10. That increased to $20 and the upward trend leveled off at $100. The most I ever received was from a wedding following my retirement from Bethany Christian in 1991. I received $100 from the couple, another $100 from the Bride's parents and yet another $100 from the Groom's parents.

I remember well a small wedding performed at the parsonage at Carlisle, Ky. Money at the preacher's house was tight and my wife looked forward to the wedding fee to supplement expenses for her planned trip to New Jersey to visit her parents. After that particular wedding, the groom departed to the car with his new bride without offering to pay me. He then abruptly returned to the front door and asked what he owed me. I replied in my usual manner: "I don't make a charge–whatever you think she's worth to you." With that, he turned around and made a quick return to the car without another word or offer to pay for the service received. As would be expected, my wife was greatly disappointed.

Many weddings were private in nature, including just the bride and groom and two witnesses to the event. I remember one counseling occasion in Anderson, Indiana when the couple requested to be married at sunset in Killbuck Park. They further inquired if they could wear Mickey Mouse outfits for the occasion. Then they timidly inquired if I had a Micky Mouse suit that I could wear for the ceremony? The reply obviously was "No." Upon second thought I remembered that I had a Mickey Mouse tie and volunteered to wear it. This pleased the couple and the plans were sealed.

One outdoor wedding in Anderson was conducted in the yard of the groom's family farm house, with the reception in a temporary tent in the barnyard. The setting was perfect under a beautiful floral covered arch. A large crowd assembled and the ceremony was underway. At this point a summer storm broke loose and everyone was drenched in the downpour of rain, including the couple, the two witnesses, and me. Everyone had to tread in the mud to the reception tent. Needless to say, it was a memorable occasion.

Funerals offered challenges unlike any other ministry, but ministry to families during the time of bereavement was appreciated more than at any other time. The approach to the bereaved family is highly important. To be available before, during and after the Memorial service is paramount to ongoing relationships with the family. The emphasis in the Memorial service may differ with each minister. Some concentrate on the life of the deceased exclusively. My remarks always began with appropriate Scriptures of comfort to the family of the deceased combined with prayer. Next was the obituary reading and appropriate remarks about the deceased. Always included was the importance of a life well lived and the preparation for life after death. The occasion always offered an opportunity not only to offer comfort in their grief but to underscore the lessons to the living. Woven in each were three "R's" They were (1) Remembrance; (2) Reflections; and (3). Resolve, touching on the past, present and future. Over the years, many different and often unexpected occurrences took place at funeral services and burials at the cemetery. Some of the most tragic in my own experience are indelibly deposited in my memory bank.

When I ministered to the Carlisle Christian Church in Kentucky, the Mortician at the Funeral Home was a member of the church. He loved to tell jokes and engage in laughter just prior to the funeral service, often making it difficult to be in the proper mood for the memorial service. . Because he was a member of the church, he assumed he could schedule funerals that

I was requested to preach by sending the notice into the Lexington paper, stating that I was the minister in charge. without personally contacted me. This worked up until the time I was scheduled to preach a funeral at a funeral home in neighboring Paris, Kentucky. The morning paper arrived announcing me as the preacher for a funeral in both Carlisle and Paris on the same day and the same time. I had no more read the obituaries in the paper than the phone rang. It was my funeral director friend in Carlisle. The message was quite simple. "O.K. I'll get someone else to do the funeral here" and he slammed down the phone.

At one funeral service the body arrived at the funeral home in Kentucky from an Eastern State just minutes prior to the scheduled funeral. The man had been murdered by his wife and the service began with the soloist singing, "When I come to the end of a perfect day."

The most inappropriate song that could have been chosen for such a tragic murder. The family was admittedly upset over the unwise choice of songs.

One of the most memorable occasions took place at the Memorial Gardens in Anderson, Indiana. The burial was the father of a high profile son in law in the city and a member of a large family. Upon arrive at the grave side, the casket was placed on two two-by-fours spanning the open grave. Since the ground was saturated from heavy rains we recognized a problem situation. Following my committal and the presentation of the flag by veterans to the widow, the saturated sod caused the support timbers to give way and the casket plunged headfirst into the grave that was filled with water. Immediately there were screams by the family members as muddy water splashed into the air. Total chaos ensued. The funeral director, for the first time in history, was at a loss what to do next. Consulting with me, we decided the family should be returned to their cars until the casket was retrieved, the corpse examined, and the whole situation rectified. The family agreed to the suggestion as long as I remained to oversee the operation. The end result of this fiasco was a lawsuit against the cemetery in which everyone of us involved were interviewed. The widow was appropriately awarded a large payment for the distress.

Another tragic event occurred after a funeral service en route to the cemetery. Before reaching the cemetery, the police car leading the procession suddenly stopped and the officer began running back to the vehicles behind us. We were forced to stop, and the driver of the hearse with whom I was riding, jumped out of the vehicle and starting running back behind us also. I then decided that maybe I should follow suit. It was only then that I saw that the family car was missing. Upon further search I discovered that the family car was off the road on its side in the ditch. Only after the driver and passengers were safely pulled out of the car did we discover that the driver had fallen asleep at the wheel. The rescued family members were distributed to other cars in the procession and we proceeded to the cemetery while the vacated car was left for a wrecker to remove. The driver who was an owner partner of the funeral home was duly lectured by his wife upon returning to the funeral home. She indicated that the incident would guarantee that they would never have another funeral with the family. The family lived in our housing addition, and her prophecy was unfulfilled. The bad experience with the burial of the husband was forgiven and the wife's service years later was handled by the same funeral service and I conducted the service.

Children of ministers are often accused of being the most out of control by church members. My response to the speculation was "If that is the case, it's because they play with the deacon's kids." The kids' mother and I both tried to instill in the hearts and minds of our four "perfect" children that they should demonstrate proper behavior at all times, not because they were preacher's kids but because they followed the norm of acceptable behavior. They rarely gave either of us cause for great concern. I do remember, however an incident that concerned David when we ministered at Carlisle, Ky. The County cemetery was directly across a deep valley from our housing development. On one occasion when I arrived at the grave side for a committal , I spotted my younger son, David, who was about 8 years of age, and his young playmate sitting on the fence overlooking the grave site. While the family and friends were exiting their vehicles, I stepped over and asked David what he was doing there. His reply was, "I just want to see what you do over here so often." I lectured him and his friend to leave and go home and that he shouldn't be there in plain view of the families and friends. He remained defiantly throughout the entire committal before leaving. Needless to say, he was properly disciplined at home that evening.

While we were ministering at Carlisle, Kentucky, we had an annual Youth Sunday when the youth were in charge of the whole service. Our oldest son, Larry, was asked to preach. It was his first experience to stand behind the pulpit and speak. As he followed his prepared notes, the fan, which was positioned behind him, blew his notes from the pulpit and scattered them on the floor a few feet below the pulpit area. Unrestrained, he promptly moved down to the lower level, gathered up his notes, and proceeded to deliver his message amidst hilarious laughter by the congregation. That was the beginning of his ongoing desire to enter the ministry and follow in the steps of his father. His younger brother, David, was to have the same experience in later years in Anderson in preparing and delivering his first sermon. He worked for days on the script but in a trial run it lasted only ten minutes. After several attempts at lengthening the sermon notes, he threw up his hands and concluded that he would give a fifteen minute invitation at the end to extend the time.

On a very special day in the 70's at the Bethany Christian Church, our son, Larry, requested to be ordained to the ministry. During the ordination I explained that Larry had been offered to the Lord at birth, because he was, in reality, a gift from the Lord. Kathryn was not supposed to become pregnant with him, having experienced a miscarriage in her first pregnancy. David, our second son, who was seated in the audience beside his mother, whispered: "I hope you didn't offer me to the Lord." Larry was later to be hired on the staff as the Minister to Youth. This arrangement was unheard of within our brotherhood, but the search committee reluctantly recommended him. The relationship lasted fifteen years up to my retirement. Being the first to have a father and son on the church staff brought many inquires from across the Nation as to my recommendation for such an arrangement. The answer was always the same: "That depends upon you and your son as to whether you can make a success of it."

At the height of the Anderson ministry, I was the Senior minister and the support staff included ministers of shepherding, adult education, children's ministry, music, finance and summer interns, as well as secretary, building maintenance person and custodian.

The elders were always thoughtful and appreciative of our leadership and on numerous occasions honored us. Some were a three-weeks trip overseas, a Cruise to Alaska, personal gifts, plaques of appreciation, etc. On a special "Lanis Kineman" Day, my wife and I were roasted by the elders with most comments directed toward my wife who was a super partner in our ministry. One elder commented in one recognition that Kathryn was an angel. The other elder responded with "What do you mean?" His reply was: "She's always up in the air preaching about something." The congregation seemed to agree.

One of the memorable experiences during our ministry at Carlisle, Ky. involved a quick trip to the Johnson Bible College Homecoming held in February.

One of our elders had died and the funeral service was postponed to allow us to attend the Homecoming and return for the service. Winters can be fierce in the Midwest during February. Snow and ice covered the roads prior to our return from Tennessee . In London, Kentucky we were turned back twice by the State Police due to the treacherous road condition between London and Mt. Vernon, Ky. We were driven to get back to Carlisle for the upcoming funeral. so we got through the blocked highway only to be caught in a pile up of cars and trucks. We soon realized that we were there for the night.

Both restaurants were out of food and overcrowded. We spent the entire night in our car with the engine running to keep warm. Naturally, we ran out of gas before daybreak. We had no cash on us but were pulled out the next morning by wrecker service without charge because we were part of the congestion on the highway. Fortunately we were pulled to a gas station where we filled the tank with credit card. Due to the bad road condition we proceeded to Mt. Vernon to a friend's house where we took time to sleep. In the meantime we were unable to arrive back in our town for the funeral. The local Methodist minister was kind enough to preach the funeral sermon. We learned the lesson well. "If anything can go wrong, it usually will." Romans 8:28 supercedes the former.

In concluding this chapter, I am reminded of the old adage: "Blessed is the man who has nothing to say and doesn't say it." That may be true of jokes that many preachers tell from the pulpit. Some may be appropriate in getting the attention of the congregation while others may seem inappropriate by others. At the risk of going over the top, I will undertake to share some of my favorites that have resonated with the congregations over the years.

The guest speaker in the pulpit, in an effort to clarify to any visitors that he was only a visiting speaker, announced: "I'm not the regular pastor this morning, I'm substituting for the regular one. To explain the situation, allow me to use the following comparison: 'If a window pane is broken and a temporary replacement with cardboard is put in place, that would describe me today.'" He proceeded to deliver a moving message. At the close of the service as he greeted the people exiting the building, a nice lady, trying to compliment him on his message declared, "You were no substitute, Sir, you were a real pain."

A minister attended a minister's meeting to hear a special speaker on an occasion. The speaker began his talk with his favorite story: "I spent the best years of my life in the arms of another man's wife, my MOTHER." The visiting minister was fascinated with the story and decided to use it in his sermon the next Sunday. "Friends" he said, "I want you to know that I spent the best years of my life in the arms of another man's wife" and then his mind went blank as he blurted out "and for the life of me I can't remember who it was."

A young man married his life-long sweetheart. In most ways they were very compatible except for the fact that she was Roman Catholic and he was a non-believer. She constantly harassed him to go to her church confession booth and talk to the priest. He resisted the repeated request stating that he was not a Catholic, and besides that, he had nothing to confess to him. Finally, to please her he agreed to go. Upon entering the booth, the priest inquired why he was there. He explained that he came because of the pressures of his wife but had nothing he wanted to confess. The priest assured him that if he sat for awhile and thought about it, he might think of something. There was a long silence. The young man finally responded that he had stopped at a construction site one afternoon on his way home from work and picked up some discarded pieces of lumber, took them home, and built a bird house. The priest's response was that the scrap lumber would have been discarded anyway, so he had made good use of throw-ways. After some time, the young man spoke up again. This time he said, "I made a second stop one day at the same site and picked up some more discarded lumber and made a dog house." Again, the priest dismissed the act as not being a sin. Then the real truth came out of the mouth of the young man. He said, "I must also tell you that I stopped a third time and loaded up enough lumber in my truck to put a room on our house." With this, the priest responded by saying that he had sinned and not only was the confession of the sin necessary but that he should make RESTITUTION. The young man responded: "Father, I don't know what that is, but I think I have enough lumber left over to build it."

Chapter 6

CONFRONTING CHURCH CON FLICTS

Throughout my years of ministry, the guiding light has been Romans 8:28 which reads:

> "And we know that all things work together for good to them that love God, to them who are the called according to his purpose."

We may not fully understand the difficulties with which we are confronted at the time they occur, but ultimately we can look back and understand the purpose God had in allowing us to walk through the valley of disappointment. Like clay in the Potter's hand, we are molded and shaped by the experiences that help us to face future reverses in our endeavors. The lyrics of my favorite hymn have been the anchor for a life time of ministry. They are as follows:

In shady green pastures, so rich and so sweet. God leads His dear children along;

Where the water's cold flow bathes the weary one's feet; God leads His dear children along.

Sometimes on the mount where the sun shines so bright, God leads His dear children along.

Sometimes in the valley in darkest of night, God leads His dear children along.

Tho' sorrows befall us and Satan oppose, God leads His dear children along

Through grace we can conquer, defeat all our foes, God leads His dear children along.

Away from the mire, and away from the clay, God leads His dear children along.

Away up in glory, eternity's day, God leads His dear children along.

Some thro' the waters, some thro' the flood, Some thro' the fire, but all thro' the blood;

Some thro' great sorrow, but God gives a song, In the night season and all the day long.

– G. A. Young

Allow me to lead you through some of those learning experiences that equipped me for future challenges.

BE NOT AFRAID

We cannot see nor can we know the meaning of life's tears;
But we can trust and we can hope which conquers all our fears.
A misty veil hides what's ahead but we can trust the one who said,
Fear not, have faith, be not afraid.

– Lanis Kineman

While serving the Normanda Christian Church at Tipton, Indiana, I graduated from Christian Theological Seminary, Butler University on August 3, 1956. Our 2nd son was born prior to that date at Tipton Memorial Hospital on October 27, 1953. The pulpit became open at Carlisle, Kentucky with the retirement of J. J. Whitehouse. One day after our commitment to visit the Carlisle Church, the search committee from Chesterfield, Indiana, came to visit with the invitation to try out for their vacated pulpit. Our commitment was to the first invitation. We were not prepared for the nature of the challenges facing us at Carlisle. Our trial message at the church was met with the invitation to be their next minister. We were not aware of the fragmented nature of the congregation but were willing to give it a nod. The parsonage was a huge 17 room, three story southern mansion that needed massive upgrading. After Kathryn told the committee that she would not live in the house. they promised to sell and build a new modern parsonage. Later, we were to learn the nature of the internal strife – those who were very liberal in theology, others who were ultra conservative and the larger group who were unaware of what the problem was all about. We were to discover that the search committee was equally divided. Because I had graduated from Johnson Bible College, the conservatives concluded that I must be the kind of preacher they desired. Because I received my M DIV from Butler, I had to be liberal in my theological persuasion. The middle group had no clue regarding the matter.

60

The first crisis that developed after we arrived took place the upcoming January the CWF led service that had become a tradition when the women from that group took charge of the morning worship service. When the chair-woman met with me outlining their plans to continue their practice, I inquired as to when the women of the Independent Missionary Society would have their day to lead a service, she replied, "Oh, No. They don't have a day". As a final resolution to keep peace among the ladies, I determined that the former practice would be unfair. The proposed service was discontinued. .The decision intensified the growing opposition of my leadership that spilled over into the board meetings that were dominated by the liberal elders

In the meantime I was invited to have lunch with the State Secretary of Christian Churches of Kentucky. Following the luncheon, he announced that Carlisle was one of the few County seat churches in Kentucky that was not in the Disciple organization and that they had called me to the church in order to bring them into the circle. If I would be willing to co-operate, he would place me in any pulpit I desired throughout the State. In behalf of fairness I replied: "In the first place, I was not called to the church as the new minister by the State office. I accepted the call to minister to the entire congregation and attempt to restore unity to the congregation. Secondly, to be fair, my goal was to help bring unity within the church, so we could minister effectively to and within the community. In addition, I would never accept a bribe as he had just made in regards to the ministry of the church.

The elders requested repeatedly that we support a Disciple College in Lexington, known for it's liberal teaching. I took it upon myself to write a letter of inquiry to the President relative to the teaching of the faculty regarding the deity of Christ, the bodily resurrection of Christ, etc. After three weeks I received a three page type written letter, avoiding my questions. The bottom line was that he could give an answer to any intelligent person but inferred that my questions were stupid. Furthermore, he would never ask anyone the questions I had asked. His letter was added to my files (still there till this day) in the event our support of the College surfaced again. It never did. I concluded that his attitude was similar to one I had heard from others:

"Would those who think they know it all get out of the way of those of us who do."

The apostle Paul wrote to the church at Corinth the following admonition:

"Let no man deceive himself. If any man among you seemeth to be wise in this world, let him become a fool, that he may be wise. For the wisdom of this world is foolishness with God. For it is written, He taketh the wise in their own craftiness. And again, The Lord knoweth the thoughts of the wise, that they are vain. Therefore let no man glory in men. For all things are yours: Whether Paul, or Apollos, or Cephas, or the world, or life, or death, or things present, or things to come; all are yours; And ye are Christ's and Christ is God's." (1 Corinthians 3:18-23).

Needless, to say, things began to go down hill. It was a long journey of preaching, personal visitation of the flock and education of the uninformed members of the Church The predominant members of the board were liberal and attempted to force the decisions in their favor. When the majority rejected each one, the number of liberals kept decreasing. The final straw came in a congregational meeting to determine the future of the parsonage situation. The liberals decided we should retain the old house, hoping it would prompt my resignation. However, the meeting took a different turn as a young lady stood and made a motion that the house be sold and a new parsonage be built in a new addition. There was an immediate second and the final vote of the congregation was an overwhelming "yes" to the motion.

There was an almost immediate effort on the part of the dissenters to leave the church and plant a new congregation of their liking. With the help of the State Secretary, they secretly laid plans for the move. On Mother's Day of the following year, the small group made their exit and started their own congregation. The result was like a purging and cleansing. of the church. With the new spirit of unity and peace we experienced a great revival led by Don Sharp. With a united leadership, the church continued to make great strides and has continued through the succeeding years to make an impact on the community and mission outreach. Division within the body of believers is never desired but sometimes can unite the remaining body of believers to fulfill the Lord's purpose for his people. The congregation that had its beginning with Elder Barton Stone in 1820 is still like a beacon on the hill reaching out to the community and beyond.

Once peace and progress were enjoyed by the congregation, a number of congregations reached out to my family, including First Christian Church in Lexington, Kentucky. The retiring minister desired me to replace him as the preaching minister and also become President of the small in- house Bible College. After refusing several offers, I attended the Kiamichi Clinic in Oklahoma where I talked with Kermit Pugh. He had resigned from the ministry of the Bethany Christian Church in Anderson, Indiana and desired me to follow him. The congregation had undergone a financial campaign, positioning the church for relocation and building on a five acre tract, donated by the Johns family and located across the street from Highland

High School.

Upon returning to Carlisle I received a phone call requesting an interview with the eldership of the Bethany Christian Church. . I complied reluctantly, but in the end accepted their call. Our family moved to Anderson in August, 1962. There had been some opposition to the financial campaign and the plans to relocate the church to the corner of Rangeline and Cross Street. Following a year of mending fences and finalizing building plans, we broke ground with the use of a walking plough. Leaders and elders pulled the rope that pulled the plow for the ground breaking in 1963 to start construction the first unit of the new building complex. The first unit was followed by the construction of an educational building to house the growing Bible School classes and offices. The construction of a Family Life Center was to follow that a few years later. The staff grew in proportion to the membership which included Senior Minister, Ministers of Music, Education, Shepherding, Youth, Children, Custodians, Maintenance Superintendent and Secretaries. The congregation was blessed with peace and harmony in the leadership and advancement was made in numerical growth, establishing new congregations and recruiting young people for ministry. Bonds were sold to finance a new worship center and other goals were put on the table including a Retirement home for elderly preachers and missionaries; a youth center, another new church plant, etc. The goals became a challenge that created differences within the leadership .Too many project attempts simultaneously created internal strife within the Board. In the midst of these plans the elders met off campus and decided to fire the music minister for insubordination, and called me to say that I needed to submit a list of complaints about his behavior to the congregation. The announced decision to the congregation only added fuel to the fire of opposition by the personal sympathizers of the music minister in a congregational meeting. As conflicts heightened there was a motion to have all ministers to resign.

My wife and I considered whether to remain with the church or accept a call we had received from a church in Knoxville, Tennessee. Some of the elders, desiring that we remain in place, asked that we agree to a confidence vote by the congregation. After much prayer, we agreed and the vote was 90% of the congregation asking us to stay. We decided that it was better to face problems than to run from them. However, this result displeased the opposition and the dissident group left the church to start another congregation. . We were faced with many uninformed and troubled members and a loss of some leaders. Our only way forward was to regroup, replace some of the leadership vacancies, and proceed with the ministry of the church. Our former experience with the Carlisle church had prepared us, to some degree, for the disappointments we encountered.

Early on in the Anderson ministry, we were faced with the decision of removing the listing of the church in the Disciples yearbook due to the Restructure of the brotherhood based upon a new Provisional design that placed the churches under a general Minister. The congregation had voted to do so, and our church was a part of some million members of Disciples churches who did the same. A new Directory of Independent churches emerged. Our church was added to the Independent Christian Church Directory.

With new leadership in some areas, a harmonious membership and a concentrated effort to return to numerical and spiritual growth, the congregation voted to construct a new Family Life Center that included a gymnasium, nursery, kitchen and youth center.

We resisted the temptation to stir the waters of further discord and moved on with the Lord's work. The division did minimal damage to either group within our community and resumption of fellowship between the churches followed after a few years.

The Bethany congregation gained recognition among our churches across the nation for two innovations. In the 1970's the church was among the first across the country to be a mega church and the first to have a father & son on the church staff. I was personally blessed to conduct leadership and church growth seminars across the Midwest in Michigan, Indiana, Ohio, Kentucky and Tennessee. My traveling companion for many of these was my dear elder friend, Ralph Brumfield, who spoke in behalf of elder leadership. My wife, Kathryn, and I were blessed with twelve more years at the church before retirement in 1991.

Two scriptures encouraged us throughout this period of time. Romans 8:28 "And we know that all things work together for good to them that love God , to them who are called according to his purpose, and 1 Cor. 15:57,58–"But thanks be to God, which giveth us the victory through our Lord Jesus Christ. Therefore, my beloved brethren, be ye steadfast, unmoveable, always abounding in the work of the Lord, forasmuch as ye know that your labour is not in vain in the Lord."

The greatest blight to church growth today is division within the body of Christ. Conflict among the members retards the outreach of the congregation and can nullify the efforts of the leadership. False charges lodged against the minister can, not only terminate his ministry with the congregation but in many cases can result in the destruction of his ministry altogether, causing him to seek secular work. Young unsuspecting preachers need to be aware of potential pitfalls that could undercut their faith and neutralize their efforts. . I recall the statement of the chairman of our church board, when backbiting among the leadership prevailed. His wise observation was "We have quit loving one another."

When the members of the Corinthian Church, in the Apostle Paul's day, engaged in internal bickering, he addressed the problems with I Corinthians 13. He concludes that chapter with the words: "And now abideth faith, hope and love; but the greatest of these is love" (13:13).

In view of possible conflict, I have reluctantly included this chapter in my presentation. To be forewarned may help to keep the peace among leaders and members of the church.

First of all, allow me to share my editorial in the BETHANY CHRISTIAN following the overwhelming vote of the people for my wife and me to stay with the church.

WE ARE STAYING

"TRUST in the Lord with all thine heart and LEAN NOT unto thine own understanding. In all thy ways ACKNOWLEDGE him and he shall DIRECT thy paths." (Proverbs 3:5,6).

That there has been turmoil within our church family is common knowledge at this point. Our leadership has been divided, each side feeling strongly that their cause was right and their actions justifiable. Because of this, a congregational vote was requested (by me) indicating confidence or lack of confidence in my leadership. The ballot was strongly worded so there would be no mistake about the wishes of our people. The request was not to give dictatorial powers to me, the preacher, but to endorse the leaders who have supported my ministry. There was no other conceivable way to break the deadlock. Since preachers are called by the congregation and elders and deacons are elected to serve by the people, it was imperative that they have a voice in this critical matter. You, the people, have spoken and we abide by your decision as reflecting the will of God.

It is true that we received a call from a very fine congregation subject to our final decision in the matter. After much prayer in which we sought earnestly the Lord's will, my wife and I have consented to stay in Anderson for the present time. As we regroup our work force and reshuffle our programs, we desire to set the stage for a united leadership within which the Holy Spirit may work and a consecrated fellowship of believers where his glory may be once again be manifested. In an effort to follow the Lord's will, there is no place for vindictive action nor slanderous language in our dealings with one another. There is a great need for all of us to forgive and ask forgiveness of one another for healing to be effected. The church family is not unlike the human family in that differences and misunderstandings arise demanding humility, confrontation and reconciliation. The secret lies in our text above which contains the wise exhortation of Solomon. The Lord is the source of our wisdom, our strength and our direction for life.

The question has been raised, "Where do we go from here?" There is only one course of action. We must return to the basics of evangelizing, teaching, shepherding and ministering to one another. All of this can be done only through the power Christ offers. Lip service is not sufficient as long as there are people hurting within the family of God and a lost world out there going to hell without the redemptive message of Christ. There are many positions to be filled and needs to be met. Will you make known your willingness to be used of the Lord in the ongoing work of His Kingdom? We trust that many will respond to the call. We look forward to seeing all of you at either the 9 or 10:15 a.m. worship service Sunday. The "Fundamentals of the Faith" class for new members or prospective members will begin Sunday Night at 5:45 p.m. in the parlor being taught by yours truly. There will be six sessions and we would be pleased to have any persons present desiring to study the fundamental doctrines of the church.

THE PERCEIVED ADVERSE EFFECTS OF A DECISION TO RESIGN AMIDST CONFLICT. (Our decision to stay with the congregation was not a selfish motive; It would have been easier to move on to greener pastures where opportunity was waiting.)

1. The deadlock between two hostile group of leaders would have perpetuated a continued battle between the two groups, destroying the unity of the body of believers.

2. I had preached through the years that problems should be confronted and worked through rather than run from.

3. To allow a small dissident group to successfully "fire" the preacher could establish a precedent within the church body of doing the same to succeeding ministers.

4. To have left would have rewarded the trouble makers by giving them success in firing the preacher over the wishes of the majority.

5. Our leaving would have undermined my own integrity before the community and left no opportunity to redeem myself against the character assassination of my opponents.

6. Complying with the demands of a few that I resign would have done irreparable damage to my family by uprooting them needlessly at an

important juncture in their young lives.

7. Many more innocent Christians would have had their faith shaken in church leadership and perhaps lost to the Kingdom forever.

8. Many of the unfinished projects that might not have been brought to fruition with our premature departure.

*The ensuing 12 years before retirement were some of the best years experienced by the church and my family.

From my own experience in dealing with conflicts, I would advise any minister who is faced with dismissal from a congregation under false accusations to consider the following advice:

1. Endeavor to bring the problem out in the open to the members rather than sweep it under the rug. People have a right to know when troublemakers become self-serving at the expense of the minister's departure.

2. Be firm in dealing with the leadership. Stand up to "ruling elders" and dissidents in a kindly manner.

3. Seek reconciliation with the alienated with a forgiving spirit.

4. Accept the support of friends within the leadership and congregation in dealing with the problems.

5. Pray for your enemies by name.

6. In the event some leave the church to start a new congregation, resist the urge to get even and definitely refrain from gossip and name-calling.

7. Forgive injustices endured and work at healing wounds and building bridges of understanding once more. (People are lonely because they build walls instead of bridges).

8. Don't allow mistreatment experienced from some leaders influence your attitudes toward all leaders of the church.

ABOVE ALL, FORGIVE AND TRY TO FORGET THE NEGATIVE PAST AND MOVE ON INTO THE FUTURE WITH RENEWED DEDICATION TO DO THE LORD'S WILL.

POSITIVE RESULTS IN THE AFTERMATH OF THE DIVISION IN 1979

1. The split restored unity to the leadership and membership of the church.

2. It resulted in many "spectators" in the stands becoming participants in the ministry arena.

3. It brought about a closer tie between the members and leaders with greater appreciation for the fellowship they experienced.

4. The split resulted in two congregations carrying out the Great

Commission in the local community and around the world. Another new congregation had been on the drawing board at Bethany prior to the separation that took place.

5. The leadership became even more focused on evangelism and ministry than even before.

6. It enabled the congregation to find ways to effect reconciliation with the departed brethren and practice love and forgiveness to others who had sown seeds of discord and division among the brethren.

7. A by-product was the generous gift of the lovely parsonage to our family, several years prior to my retirement.

8. The congregation became more mission minded with the institution of a Faith Promise to send our son, Larry and his family, along with timothy Tom Foust and family to England as church planters under the auspice of Christian Missionary Fellowship This was in addition to the Mission budget in place.

TO GOD BE THE GLORY; GREAT THINGS HE HAS DONE. (Romans 8:28 still in effect)

Shortly after our retirement from Bethany in 1991, we moved to Phoenix, Arizona and were providentially offered the opportunity to lead a ministry to seniors at the Chandler Christian Church, Roger Storms, Minister. During this tenure I lost my beloved wife, Kathryn, of forty-six years, during surgery in Indianapolis, Indiana. Then to First Christian Church in Sun City as Outreach Minister. I was married after two years to Vanda Rodgers, a former student of Johnson Bible College. She served with me for three years at Sun City Christian Church. We were asked to accept a preaching ministry to a new congregation in Wickenburg, Az. After three years with little progress of building plans, we resigned. With the sudden death of Vanda, I answered the call to be Minister of Seniors at the Paseo Verde Christian Church in Peoria, Az. I ministered 6 ½ years before retiring in June, 2011.In the meantime, I met Nancy Norton at Christ Church of the Valley in Peoria, Az. and we were married in a beautiful garden wedding in Sun City, Az. on May 7, 2005. She has become the joy of my semi-retirement ministry that we have shared together. The Lord knew I needed a helpmate so he gave me a third Christian helpmeet. It is my prayer that these reflections may be the source of encouragement, whether one is in the valley of trials or the mountain of triumph.

Every preacher should take the opportunity of REFLECTING ON THE PAST, RENEWING ONE'S FAITH IN THE PRESENT AND RESOLVING TO STAND IN THE FUTURE.

As mortals with feet of clay, we make mistakes but the Lord's forgiveness and inner strength by the Holy Spirit enables us to be encouraged by the apostle Paul's challenge to the church in Galatia recorded in 5:25,26: "If we live in the Spirit, let us also walk in the Spirit. Let us not be desirous of vain glory, provoking one another, envying one another."

COPING WITH CHANGE IN THE CHURCH

Our world is changing from isolated continents to a neighborhood with today's advancement in technology. The church procedures in methodology are changing. Paul said, "I have become all things to all men so that by all possible means I might save some." (1 Cor. 9:22b).

I.   CHANGE WITHIN OUR CHURCHES HAS ALREADY BEGUN.

    A. The number of Mega churches is increasing.
    B. The number and variety of worship experiences are changing.
    C. Church music is changing.
    D. Approach to preaching is changing.
    E. Youth ministry is changing.
    F. Church structures are changing.
    G. The way to raise money to do the Lord's work is changing.
    H. Church leaders are under pressure to make changes in these areas.

II. GENERATIONAL FACTORS IN CHANGE.

    A. Five generations can be found in the church today.
    B. The generations have varying characteristics.
        1. The Patriotic generation (Born 1910-1927)
        2. The Unique generation (Born 1928–1942)
        3. The Liberated generation (Born 1943-1955)
        4. A new Conservative generation (Born 1956-1970)
        5. The Next generation (Born 1968-2000)
    C. THE MEANING OF GENERATIONAL THEORY.
        1. It helps to explain some of the conflict in churches over values, priorities, purpose and resource allocation.
        2. It explains why what works with one generation does not work with another.
        3. It contributes to our understanding of why several people drop out or leave the church when there is a change in ministers.
        4. It explains the difficulty of cross generational ministry.
        5. It explains why a 57 year old senior minister does not understand youth ministry.

6. It explains why most adults get along with those older than we are but not those younger than we are.
7. It explains why older ministers sometimes have trouble understanding young ministers on their staffs.
8. It explains why older professionals who must communicate with younger people often move into management.
9. It explains the need for bridge generations.
10. It is explained by the deference pyramid.
    a. younger defer to older.
    b. newcomers defer to those with longer tenure.
    c. women defer to men.
    d. employees defer to employers
    e. less educated to more educated
    f. those without titles defer to those with titles
    g. lower end of the salary scale to high end
    h. those from small institutions defer to those from large
    i. Blacks, Asians and Hispanics to Anglos
    j. students to teacher
    k. laity to clergy
11. It helps to explain why the ministry is so difficult today.

– Lyle E. Schaller

Dr. Robert Schuller, pastor of the Garden Grove Community Church in California has shared the following insights:

"The preacher's job is to keep in mind roles, goals and tolls. You must define your role before you set your goal." Growth must be planned. If there is vital life, there must be continued growth. Just as soon as you get this continued growth, life is going to run into growth restricting obstacles. As a child grows, he runs into obstructions. Clothes and shoes get too small. The shoe must never tell the foot <u>how</u> big to get. Never surrender leadership to the shoe. Growth obstructions must be removed to keep them from dictating to leadership. The fundamental problem of leadership is to remove man made growth restricting obstacles that keep God from making the thing as big as He wants it."

Chapter 7

SERMONS THAT RESONATE

In preaching, the obvious tool is the Bible, the Word of God. The starting point of preaching is preparation from the Word and inspiration by the Holy Spirit. Concentrated research, bathed in prayer, are also imperative in sermon preparation. Courses in Homiletics and Hermeneutics are introductory courses the preacher should have had in his College studies. Paul sets forth vital information in his admonition to young Timothy as follows: "All scripture is given by inspiration of God, and is profitable for doctrine, for reproof, for correction, for instruction in righteousness: that the man of God may be perfect, thoroughly furnished unto all good works." (2 Timothy 3:16,17). The sermon should be Bible based, Christ centered and People oriented.

Many Scriptural verses throughout the New Testament are what we might say are oxymorons. Our everyday language often contains them, when we say " sweet sorrow" or "thunderous silence". Paul says in 2 Corinthians 5:17: "If any man be **in Christ** he is a new creature; old things are passed away; behold, all things are become new" In his letter to the Colossians, he writes: "To whom God would make known what is the riches of the glory of this mystery among the Gentiles; which is **Christ in you**, the hope of glory" (Colossians 1:27). The skeptic might see the two different statements as being contradictory while they actually picture the change that takes place in the spiritual growth of the convert. Take for instance the picture of the old country blacksmith. He first puts the iron in the fire after which the fire is in the iron. As Christians, we first put on Christ by faith and obedience to His commands. After we grow in our faith, we are inspired and energized by the Holy Spirit, Christ is in us.

Jesus is our teacher. Throughout the Gospels He teaches us: How to live, how to die and how to live again. He alone is the Way, the Truth and the Life. Without Him, the Way, there is no going; without Him, the Truth, there is no knowing; without Him, the Life, there is no living.

Sermon preparation and presentation come in different formats; some fly while others seem to disconnect with the congregation. However, after the times I seemed to have struck out, someone would comment at the exit after the service, "Thanks, preacher, your message was just what I needed this morning." The success of any message is in the mind and need of the listener.

My favorite style of preaching through the years has used alliteration for the main points. It enabled my presentation to run more smoothly and made it easier for the listener to absorb the message. The seeds for many messages came many times when I was awakened in the middle of the night with thoughts of a particular subject. If I did not immediately arise and record the inspired points, they were forgotten and lost forever. Of course, the bottom line is that people want to see a sermon in the life of the messenger, in addition to hearing the message.

Sermons, in addition to being Scriptural, can be prepared and delivered as seasonal occasion, exegetical, evangelistic or topical. in nature. The following sermons delivered over the years are two of my favorites. The first is a basic sermon on the nature of God's will for us and the nature of our own personal wills.

IT'S A MATTER OF THE WILL

"I can do all things through Christ which strengtheneth me."
(Philippians 4:13) (James 4:13-17). KJV.

INTRODUCTION:

Several years ago when Johnny Carson returned to the Tonight show after being away for some time, he began by boasting with the phrase: "I am your PERMANENT host." This, of course, could be taken as reckless boasting since there is nothing permanent in this life. James admonishes with the words:

For what is your life? It is even a vapour, that appeareth for a little time, and then vanisheth away. For that ye ought to say, If the Lord will, we shall live, and do this or that." (James 4:14,15).

Or consider the parable of Jesus about the rich farmer in Luke 12, who was rebuked by God for his selfish interest in building more barns for bigger crops in a show of selfish indulgence over the accumulation of things. God declared: "This night thy soul shall be required of thee and whose shall these things be? All of our plans in life should be prefaced with the words, "If the Lord wills."

> "Today is mine; tomorrow may not come.
> I may not see the rising of the sun;
> When evening falls, my work may all be done;
> Today is mine, tomorrow may not come."

A young father or mother reasons, "When I finish my project or excel in my career, I'll spend more time with the kids." Time passes quickly and the kids are grown and out of the nest with no opportunity to fulfill their plans. A couple says, "When we retire, we're planning to travel or engage in a mission project" Retirement comes and with it an unexpected illness or early death. Plans forfeited!

In the planning of our lives, two realities should be kept in delicate balance. They are: 1. God's sovereignty and 2. Man's free will. To do so, one must understand God's plan and purpose in creating man in the beginning. We read in Genesis 1:26 "Then God said, 'Let us make man in our image, in our likeness and let them rule over the fish of the sea and the birds of the air; over the livestock, over all the earth and over all the creatures that move along the ground'.

Since God is Spirit (John 4:24) and man is flesh and blood, how are we made in His image? Since we read that man is created in his likeness, what is man? Genesis 1:26 says, "And God said, 'Let us make man in our image, after our likeness: and let them have dominion over the fish of the sea, and over the fowl of the air, and over the cattle, and over all the earth, and over every creeping thing that creepeth upon the earth. "So God created man in his own image, in the image

Of God created he him; male and female created he them".We understand the Godhead to be Father, Son and the Holy Spirit. Man, in the beginning, was created body, soul and spirit. With the body we relate to the world around us; with the soul we relate to ourselves and with the spirit we relate to God. Paul alludes to this makeup of man in 1 Thessalonians 5:23b: "May your whole spirit, soul and body be kept blameless at the coming of our Lord Jesus Christ." The question remains:

How are we made in the image of God? When he created man he gave him the same abilities that He possesses: the ability to think, feel and will. Man is capable of blushing, to exercise authority over His creation and to make decisions. While God is Sovereign, He has given to man the ability to exercise his free will. The obvious result of this was the fiasco in the Garden of Eden. The first couple made the wrong choice and were driven from the

Garden. They chose to listen to Satan instead of God.

In consideration of the will of God, we would better understand it in three dimension. 1. God's **Intentional** will was announced in the beginning, but man's responsive will changed everything. Once the first couple were expelled from the beautiful garden,.God's **Circumstantial** will came into play. Man's continued disobedience produced relationships that God did not intend but were tolerated.

His **Ultimate** will is that, through Christ, all men might come to repentance and be saved.

For a clearer understanding of man's will we have broken it down in three categories:

I.   I WILL IF I CAN–**DISCOVERY.**
II.   I CAN IF I WILL–**DETERMINATION.**
III.   I CAN IF GOD WILLS–**DEDICATION.**

I.   I. WILL IF I CAN–**DISCOVERY**.

A. For you are God's workmanship, created in Christ Jesus to do good works, which God prepared in advance for us to do." (Eph. 2:10).

B. "It was he who gave some to be apostles, some to be prophets, some to be evangelists, some to be pastors and some to be teachers, to prepare God's people for works of service so that the body of Christ may be built up, until we all reach unity in the faith and in the knowledge of the Son of God and become mature, attaining to the whole measure of the fullness of Christ." (Eph. 4:11-13).

C. God has endowed each of us with certain abilities and when we became Christians we were endowed with certain spiritual gifts to perform the ministry of Christ and build up the body of Christ, the church--DISCOVERY. Each person must find the areas in which he or she is gifted. Some have the gift to sing, others to play instruments, other, to encourage; others to be good stewards; some to speak fluently; some to do manual tasks, etc. The performance should be in proportion to the qualification.

As the story goes: A young man who was physically and mentally challenged, accepted the Lord and asked his pastor for a job. He was directed to the church secretary who gave him some church letter heads, envelopes, postage and a list of delinquent church members to contact. Time passed and the minister received a letter from a prominent doctor in the congregation. Tucked inside the letter was a check for $5,000. He apologized for being a delinquent member and added a P.S. "Please tell your secretary that there is only one "I" in dirty and no "c" in skunk. The letter of the young man was not written in proper language but did get results in this instance. In discovering one's gift, there must be the recognition of limitations as well as ability. There is also the danger of not being satisfied with one's present ministry and desiring to have what someone else has.

An elderly man was having coffee at his favorite restaurant. The waitress observed that he put three heaping spoons of sugar in his coffee and asked for more. The waitress responded to the request by saying: "Bud, you can't have any more sugar until you stir what you already have."

Paul wrote to young Timothy "Wherefore I put these in remembrance, that thou stir up the gift of God, which is in thee by the putting on of their (elders) hands" (2 Timothy 1:6). We have different gifts, according to the grace given us." (Romans 12:6).

II.   I CAN IF I WILL–**(DETERMINATION)**.

Our ability must be matched by our availability and our accountability. Ability is useless unless it is put into action and each must be able to give an account to God for the things we do.

> "Isn't it strange that princes and kings and
> Clowns that caper in sawdust rings;
> And common folk like you and me,
> Are builders of eternity;
> To each is given a bag of tools,
> A shapeless mass and a book of rules;
> And each must fashion 'ere life is flown;
> A stumbling block or a stepping stone."

The bottom line is that our common gifts must be exercised with an uncommon determination. Right goals must be matched with strong wills.

The apostle Paul wrote to the church at Corinth, "I was determined to know nothing among you save Jesus Christ and Him crucified" (1 Cor. 2:2).

Commitment is a rare quality these days. The church is not exempt from this problem. In the marriage experience, many prefer to live in without any commitment. In the church there are those who choose to be attenders and not members. Attenders become consumers while members are contributors. The scriptures clearly point out that we are called out of the world into a spiritual body of believers with shared responsibilities. Salvation and fellowship are twin spiritual experiences joined at the head and the heart. In conversion we are joined to Christ; in membership of the church we are connected to the body of believers. In our commitment to use the gifts God has given us, we must also determine whether our involvement is a Job or a Ministry.

A lukewarm male Christian once moaned as he evaluated his connection to the church of his choice. His evaluation went something like this: "In my first visit to church, the preacher tried to drown me in the baptistery." In the second visit, "he tied me up to a woman." When I go the third time, "they'll probably throw dirt on me."

Relationships have to be nurtured and spiritual ties within the body of Christ also have to be developed. Someone has described their take on the fellowship within the church in the following lines:

> "To dwell above with the saints we love;
> O that will be glory;
> To dwell below with the saints we know;
> Well that's another story."

Chuck Swindoll gives his view on differences that exist in church fellowships: "The church is like a nest of porcupines–the closer they get together the more they needle each other." One thing of which we can be sure: Christian maturity is reached only by the proper diet (Word of God) and the proper exercise (Worship and Ministry). James' admonition is "Anyone then who knows to do good and doesn't do it sins."(James 4:17).

III.   I CAN IF GOD WILLS–(**DEDICATION**).

There are three different parts to God's will and must be taken into consideration when we seek His will for our lives:

1. **His intentional will**–what He performs – Creation.

2. **His circumstantial will**–what He permits – Fall of man.

3. **His ultimate will**–what He prefers – Redemption.

What God performs is clear from Scripture. God has acted in history and the future is secure, as the Lyrics of a much loved hymn by Maltrie D. Babcock states:

> "This is my Father's world,
> O let me ne'er forget;
> That though the wrong seems oft so strong,
> God is the ruler yet.

This is my Father's world,
The battle is not done,
Jesus who died shall be satisfied;
And heaven and earth be one."

God's intention for man in the creation was for fellowship. He was placed in a beautiful surrounding, designed for a permanent abode and relationship with Him.

His intentional will was unfulfilled with man's surrender to Satan's deceptive promises.

Therefore, we must remember that many things that happen to us in an imperfect world may not be the direct act of God at all, but what He permits in the face of our weaknesses. Satan is very much alive in our world and is the spoiler of man. The book of Job is a striking example of God permitting Satan to test Job's commitment to Him through a series of adversities. Many of the things that happen to us in this life may be the result of our own bad choices. Natural disasters and evil rulers may be permitted by God to get our attention and lead us back on the right path.

God's ultimate will is seen through the sacrifice of His only begotten son to reconcile us to Him. His backup plan was conceived from the foundation of the world as the New Testament story unfolds. (John 3:16). The history of God's dealings with man throughout the Old Testament reveals His plan in choosing a Nation that would be separate and apart from other nations in preparation for the advent of Jesus Christ, His only Begotten Son.

Anything God cannot do is a limitation imposed by His nature, not His power. Bad things often happen to good people; however Romans 8:28 makes it clear that God is able in His ultimate will to cause all things to work out for the good of those who love Him and desire to be in the center of His Ultimate will.

Peter, in his second epistle (2 Peter 3:8,9) writes: But do not forget this one thing, dear friends: With the Lord a day is like a thousand years, and a thousand years are like a day. The Lord is not slow in keeping his promise, as some understand slowness. He is patient with you, not willing that any should perish, but everyone to come to repentance."

Finally, Paul writes in Romans 12:1,2: "Therefore, I urge you brothers, in view of God's mercy, to offer your bodies as living sacrifices, holy and pleasing to God. This is your spiritual act of worship. Do not conform any longer to the pattern of this world but be transformed by the renewing of your mind. Then you will be able to test and approve what God's will is–His good, pleasing and perfect will."

There are three basic guidelines to enable us to know God's will in a given situation: (1) Genuine desire to know it. (2) Learn from scripture, prayer and wise counsel. (3) Submit to it. If we do the things within God's will that we know to do, He will give further insight into other areas.

Finally, OUR DESTINY IS DETERMINED BY OUR CHOICES, NOT CHANCES.

The choice is ours: With Christ it's an endless life; Without Christ it's a lifeless end.

In a small community there lived a wise old man, known throughout the countryside for his wisdom. One day some mischievous boys decided to trick the old man. The one boy held out his closed hands and indicated that he had a bird between his hands. He posed a question: Is the bird dead or alive? The old gentleman knew that it was a trick question. He surmised that if he answered that the bird was alive, the boy would crush the bird and then instantly present it dead. If he said the bird is dead, the youth would open his hands and present the bird alive. Either way, he would be wrong. The response of the wise man was, "It is as you would have it."

God has provided an opportunity for each of us to choose between life or death.

The choice is ours. Peter writes: "The Lord is not slack concerning his promise, as some men count slackness; but is longsuffering to us-ward, not willing that any should perish, but that all should come to repentance." (2 Peter 3:9)

A special day's sermon is presented as follows:

ROADBLOCKS TO A THANKFUL HEART

(Romans 1:18-25)

The heathen world under Rome's domination never observed a Thanksgiving Day. Paul continues to explain the reason for their dilemma: "because that knowing God they glorified him not as God, neither gave thanks"-Romans 1:21.

It is a picture of the degradation into which mankind ever sinks when turning from the TRUTH OF GOD and who is no longer restrained by His grace. Thanksgiving is impossible without a true recognition of God. Both the Bible and experience teach us that thanksgiving is a gift of God because there is seemingly little correlation between one's outward circumstances and the spirit of gratitude. Paul had little for which to be thankful, humanly speaking, but he was always singing a song of thanksgiving. The Christian has every reason to be thankful because he has experienced the love of God in his life.

Paul exhorts in 1 Thessalonians 5:16-18: "In everything give thanks, rejoice always and pray continually." EVERYTHING? National emergencies, financial reverses, harassment by one's enemies, lousy weather, terminal illnesses and every kind of human perplexity? Yes! IN everything, not necessarily FOR everything. Human response to good fortune is often connected to giving thanks – a $5 bill found at the curb; rain after the seeding of the lawn or planting of crops; sunshine on our picnic or an unexpected raise in salary. Thanks becomes a kind of payment for goods received. However, the correlation between good fortune and gratitude expressed is ridiculously low.

The person most thankful for his money will not be the one who has the most but who is on a very tight budget. It is most likely the sick who are grateful for any improvement. The sorrowing are grateful for God's comforting. (Grief, by the way, is the price we pay for caring).There is a grave danger of brooding over our calamities and overlooking God's mercies. We need to cultivate the spirit of the lady who had only two teeth and was thankful that the two hit.

Thus, the people to whom Paul refers in Romans chapter 1 manifested roadblocks to a thankful heart. These were **PRIDE**, **PROSPERITY**, **PROMISCUITY** AND **PLEASURE**.

I.   THE FIRST ROADBLOCK THAT LED TO THANKLESSNESS WAS PRIDE

"Professing themselves to be wise, they became fools" (v. 22).

To the church at Corinth, Paul wrote: "For after that in the wisdom of God the world by wisdom knew not God, it pleased God by the foolishness of preaching to save them that believe." (1 Cor. 1:21).

"Pride goeth before destruction and a haughty spirit before a fall" (Prov. 16:18). Intellectual pride is always the enemy of man–self-sufficiency leads to arrogance and self-worship which is categorized as humanism (2Timothy 3:1-5).

Humanism leads to all forms of idolatry and even fetishism.

II.   PROSPERITY CAN BE A ROADBLOCK TO THANKFULNESS

"But godliness with contentment is great gain. For we brought nothing into this world and it is certain we can carry nothing out. And having food and raiment let us be therewith content. But they that will be rich fall into temptation and a snare, and into many foolish and hurtful lusts, which drown men in destruction and perdition. The love of money is the root of all evil: which while some coveted after, they have erred from the faith, and pierced themselves through with many sorrows. (1 Timothy 6:6-10). Paul further warns Timothy "For men shall be lovers of their own selves, covetous, boasters, proud, blasphemers, disobedient to parents, unthankful, unholy . . .(2 Timothy 3:2).

Most people can survive poverty better than prosperity. Affluence often breeds

selfishness but the sin of covetousness hinges on the "love of, not the possession of money." The Roman period Paul was writing about was an age of unparalleled luxury. Hot and cold water ran from silver taps in the public baths. Caligula had even sprinkled the floor of the circus arena with gold dust instead of sawdust. Seneca spoke of money as the ruin of the true honour of things . . . "not what a thing truly is but what it cost." Crime became the only antidote to boredom. Tacitus observed, "the greater the infamy, the wilder the delight." The counter to all of this luxury was displayed in the theme of a National Missionary Convention: "Christians should LIVE simply that others might SIMPLY LIVE."

III.   PROMISCUITY WAS A THIRD ROADBLOCK TO A THANKFUL HEART.

It was an age of unparalleled immorality, a lifestyle of SENSUALISM.

There had not been one single case of divorce in the first 520 years of the history of Rome. But then, as Seneca reported, "Women were married to be divorced and divorced to be married." Roman high-born matrons dated the years by the names of the consuls. Society was riddled with unnatural vice. Fourteen of the first 15 Roman Emperors were homosexuals, according to history.

IV.   A FOURTH ROADBLOCK TO THANKFULNESS WAS PLEASURE.

This was characterized as HEDONISM.

God abandoned them to uncleanness in their heart's passionate desires for pleasure; desires which made them dishonour their bodies among themselves (Vs. 24). The word translated desires is **epithumia** –reaching after pleasure that defies all reason–LUST. A passionate desire for forbidden pleasure (Remember Adam and Eve?). It was a kind of insanity that makes a man do things he would never have done if the desire had not taken away his sense of honor and decency. He becomes so immersed in his lustful desires that His awareness of God ceases altogether. The wrath of God is revealed against all such things. Wrath is the inevitable punishment for sin. Judgment is precisely the result of disobedience to God's order of the Universe. The Bible and experience also teach that whatever you sow, you reap. Poverty stricken indeed is the person who has nothing for which to be thankful.

Were thanks with every gift expressed, each day would be thanksgiving; Were gratitude its very best, Each life would be thanksliving.

Chapter 8

OVERCOMING DISCOURAGEMENT

There will be days throughout the preacher's ministry that discouragement will set in. You may feel that the world is moving too fast or reverses of plans become too numerous. How do we handle the complaints, criticisms and sometimes falsehoods thrown our way?

Once again, we need to turn to the appropriate scriptures and lean in prayer upon our Lord who faced many trials, disappointments in his followers He offers encouragement to us when we feel rejected, unneeded and misunderstood in our multifarious hours and days of ministry. One scripture that has helped me during those times is found in Philippians 4:4-9.

"**Rejoice** in the Lord always: and again I say, **Rejoice**. Let your moderation be known unto all men. The Lord is at hand. Be careful for nothing; but in every thing by prayer and supplication with thanksgiving let your requests be made known unto God. **Relate.** Be careful for nothing **Relax** but in every thing by prayer and supplication with thanksgiving let your requests be made known unto God. **Request.** And the peace of God, which passeth all understanding, shall keep your hearts and minds through Christ Jesus. Finally, brethren, whatsoever things are true, whatsoever things are honest whatsoever things are just, whatsoever things are pure, whatsoever things are lovely whatsoever things are of good report: if there be any virtue and if there be any praise, think on these things." "**Receive** . . . and the God of peace shall be with you."

Discouragement is closely related to fear. We may fear that we can't meet the expectations of our family, friends or parishioners. Fear may seize us when we stand up before the congregation to speak because we are ill prepared. Let me hasten to say that controlled fear is our friend because it prompts us to be well prepared or to take caution in risky endeavors. In the secular world, fear seems to be a cloud of doubt, suspicion, distrust, confusion and alienation like a cloud hanging over us. There, of course, are legitimate fears that prompt us to prepare and perform at our best. Proverbs 9:10 reads: "The fear of the Lord is the beginning of wisdom; and the knowledge of the holy is understanding."

Jesus said, "And fear not them which kill the body, but are not able to kill the soul: but rather fear him which is able to destroy both soul and body in hell."(Matthew 10:28).

Unhealthy, even devastating fear can immobilize us through paralysis and can curtail our effective performance at best. During a storm on the sea of Galilee while Jesus slept, the disciples were frightened and awakened him: "Lord, save us or we perish" His reply was "Why are ye fearful, O ye of little faith?" Their experience was not unlike the storms in life that we face–economic downturn, job security, health problems, domestic challenges, etc.

I.   THE CAUSE OF FEAR

Let's put it in acrostic form so that we can confront some of the causes:

F eeling forsaken by others.
E vil threats by Satan and his host of demons.
A nonimity. Secret of the unknown and unexperienced.
R ejection by others/low self esteem.

The greatest antidote to fear is trust. God is greater than our fears and anxieties.

Different instruction than the person who received the following advice: "Cheer up; things could be worse! So I cheered up and sure enough they were." (Bad outlook).

A student at one of our ivy league universities suggested to his room mate who was struggling with a problem and greatly discouraged: "Go talk to Phillip Brooks, the great preacher and he will help you with your problem. He did and upon returning was asked "What did he tell you?" "I didn't ask him", was his reply, "Spending an hour in his presence took away my problem." His experience is magnified when, in our prayer experience with the Lord, troubles always seem to disappear when we spend time in the Lord's presence, we focus upon the greatness of God.

The source of our fear is Satan himself. He is referred to in Scripture as a liar and the father of all lies. (John 8:44). He is also the discourager of the saints. The world's deadliest disease is not cancer, aids, heart problems, or MS, it is **DISCOURAGEMENT**. It is universal, can reoccur and is highly contagious. It is the first of three downward moods followed by despondency and despair. The effect of unbridled discouragement is depression. Unbridled grief may produce depression.

In 1994 my wife, Kathryn, of forty-six years, underwent surgery to replace a valve in the aorta artery at St. Vincent's Hospital in Indianapolis. What was expected to be a routine surgery exposed a heredity problem in the size of the blood vessel that made it too small for a valve. She did not survive the surgery. The months following her death led to deep depression with which I struggled for some time. I refused all medical treatment. The only answers were prayer and redirection of my ministry.

Two years later I became engaged to a former classmate at Johnson Bible College. We spent 6 1/2 years together in our marriage. We purchased a lovely home in Sun City West and moved from the Condo in Sun City. A few weeks later I announced my resignation from the Mountain View Christian Church in Wickenburg. The next day we were out shopping for a rug for the house entrance. Driving down Grand Avenue, Vanda suddenly stopped talking and went into a violent seizure. I was caught in the traffic with no phone access and plan to get her to Boswell Hospital about a mile away. A young man in a pickup truck saw what was happening in our van from his rear view mirror. He proceeded to run back to our vehicle, having surveyed the situation, he instructed me to follow him as he proceeded on the shoulder of the road past all of the stalled traffic, through red traffic lights and to the emergency room of the hospital. Having summoned a doctor and three nurses to our van who promptly carted her into the hospital. The young man, having done all that was humanly possible, assuring me he would be praying for her and me, departed without my even knowing his name. He will forever be our angel in the time of tragic circumstances. Vanda was pronounced dead on arrival. I had experienced a change of address, a resignation from the place of ministry and the death of my wife within a few weeks time. This marked the second time of grief and major loss in my life. It took some time to return to a normal lifestyle and return to ministry. A search of the scriptures encouraged me and reminded me that many biblical characters suffered from depression. Among them were Abraham (Genesis 15), Jonah (Jonah 4), Job, Elijah (I Kings 19), Saul (I Samuel 16:14-23), Jeremiah, and David (Psalm 38:51). I learned from my struggles and study of Biblical passages some insight into the nature and response to stress that leads to discouragement and ultimately depression.

II. **IDENTIFICATION**: Be in touch with WHO YOU ARE:

1. Love others as yourself.
2. Know your strengths and weaknesses.
3. Work to improve your weaknesses.
4. Accept who you are.
5. Maintain a thankful attitude.
6. Share with others you can trust.
7. Laugh a lot. Don't take yourself too seriously.
8. Learn to like what you do.

III. **DEDICATION**. Know WHOSE you are.

1. Self-sufficiency is fantasy–God's sufficiency is wisdom.
2. God has revealed answers to our problems (1 Cor. 10:1-13; Romans 15:4.)
3. Know whom you're trying to please. If you don't know you'll cave in to three things: Criticism, Competition, and Conflict.

IV. **ORGANIZATION**–Know what you want to accomplish.

1. Christ said, "I know where I came from and I know where I'm going." (John 8:14).
2. Unless you plan your life and set your priorities, you will feel pressured.
3. Preparation prevents pressure but procrastination produces it.

V. **CONCENTRATION:** Focus on one thing at a time. (Phil. 3:13-14).

1. Live one day at a time. "This is the day the Lord has made; I will rejoice and be glad in it." (Psalm 118:24).
2. Seize the opportunities to minister to people.
3. Don't let the sun go down upon your wrath. (Eph. 4:26).
4. Don't worry and fret. Jesus said it.
5. Surround yourself with friends.

VI. **DELEGATION**–Don't try to do every thing yourself.

1. Jesus chose 12 men to mentor and send out.
2. Why do we try to do everything ourselves? Perfectionism and/or insecurity.

VII. **MEDITATION** –Maintain a habit of Bible study and prayer.

1. Jesus gave us an example by his own lifestyle. (Mark   1:35).
2. Make prayer your first choice, not your last chance.
3. The secret of living is learning to pray:
   It's asking our Father for strength for the day.

It's trusting completely that His boundless grace,
Will overcome care and each problem we face.
It's walking by faith every mile that we plod,
And knowing our prayers bring us closer to God.

4. The essence of prayer is not overcoming God's reluctance but laying hold on His willingness.

VIII. **RECREATION**–Take time for relaxation and change of pace.

1. Under pressure of the crowds Jesus said to his disciples, " Come with me by yourselves to a quiet place and get some rest" (Mark 6:31).
2. Realize that no person is indispensable to a job. We can all be replaced and will be some day.

IX. **A SUMMARY OF DOS AND DON'TS IN OVERCOMING DISCOURAGEMENT AND DEPRESSION.**

A. The account of Elijah in his contest with the false prophets at Mt. Carmel with discouragement by the threat of the wicked Jezebel who threatened his life (I Kings 19:1-18).

B. Elijah felt six emotions–fear, resentment, low self-esteem, guilt, loneliness, and worry.

C. Lessons learned from Elijah's experience:
   1. Don't focus on your feelings. Face the facts. (vs. 3).
   2. Don't compare yourself to others.-"I am no better than my ancestors."
   3. Don't take all the blame for the situation (vs. 10). "The Israelites have Broken your covenant–"I am no better."
   4. Don't exaggerate the negative. (vs. 10) "I am the only one left." God Revealed 7,000 who had not bowed the knee to Baal.
   5. Do take care of your physical needs. (vv. 5-8). Eat, sleep and drink.
   6. Do share your frustration with the Lord. (vv. 9,10).
   7. Obtain a fresh awareness of God's presence in your life. (Vv. 11).
   8. Do let God give you a new direction for your life. (vv. 15) "Go back the way you came."

D. Sources of strength for our lives in times of discouragement:
   1. The plan of God–His will for our lives.
   2. The promises of God in His Word.
   3. The people of God within the body of believers.
   4. The presence of God through the Holy Spirit.

E.   Challenges to overcoming discouragement.:
1. Don't run from your problems–face them.
2. Don't fix blame–fix the problem.
3. Don't hold grudges–forgive from the heart.
4. Make friends of your enemies.
5. Spend time helping others.

X.   **THE COST OF FEAR TO OUR LIVES.**

A.   The emotional cost.

Some people fall into mental and emotional collapse because of fear. The truth is that most things we fear never happen–someone has estimated that 92%of the things we fear never happen.

Dr. S. I. McMillen says that about 9 million Americans suffer from mental illness. 1 out of every 20 Americans will have psychotic disturbance severe enough to be hospitalized.

B.   The physical cost.

It has been estimated that fear and it's resultant emotional stress account for two thirds of more of the physical illnesses today. They take the form of high blood pressure, heart trouble, kidney disease.

C. The spiritual cost of fear.

Fear stifles the Holy Spirit's effectiveness in our lives. In 1 John 4:4 the promise is given: "Greater is he that is in you than he that is in the world. "For you did not receive a spirit that makes you a slave to fear, but you received the spirit of sonship" (Romans 8:15).

Fear keeps us from being joyful, happy, radiant persons, causing us to be thankless, complaining and defeated persons.

Paul says in 2 Timothy 1:7: "For God hath not given us the spirit of fear; but of power and of love and of a sound mind."

Fear is the opposite of faith that expresses itself in trust.

XI.   **THE CURE FOR OUR FEARS.**

A.   A good place to begin is Romans 8:31. "If God be for us, who can be against us?" Too often we seek for happiness in the wrong places. The world offers pleasure that is short lived; the Lord offers us joy. Happiness comes from outward gratification while joy comes from God and is experienced within the inner person. Faith expresses TRUST, while fear produces DOUBT that in turn destroys HOPE. "And now these three remain: faith, hope and love. But the greatest of these is love." (NIV).

One evening in 1808 a gaunt sad faced man entered the office of Dr. James Hamilton in Manchester, England. The Dr. was struck by the melancholy appearance of his patient. He inquired, "What is your problem?" His response was "Dr. I am sick of a mortal malady. I am frightened of the terror in the world around me. I am depressed by life. I can find no happiness anywhere; nothing amuses me. I've nothing to live for. If you can't help me, I shall kill myself." The Dr. responded: "Your malady is not life threatening. You need only to get out of yourself; you need to laugh and get some pleasure out of life. Go to the circus tonight and see Gremaldi, the clown. He's the funniest man alive. He'll cure you."

A spasm of pain crossed the poor man's face as he said,

"Doctor, don't jest with me. I am Gremaldi."

The world is filled with Gremaldies–men and women who have tried the pleasures that the world offers not knowing the real joy and happiness that come through Him who said, "I am come that ye may have life and have it more abundantly.

Psalm 27 is a prayer attributed to David that is against three dangers:

1. Choosing our own way. "There is a way that seemeth right unto man but the end thereof are the ways of death."
2. Trusting, even in the simplest way, in our own strength and wisdom. "Trust in the Lord with all thine heart and lean not to thine own understanding. In all thy ways acknowledge Him and He shall direct thy paths."
3. Being left to our own weakness or distrusting God's leading. "But now this is what the Lord says–he who created you, O Jacob, he who formed you, O Israel: "Fear not, for I have redeemed you; I have summoned you by name; you are mine. When you pass through the waters, I will be with you; and when you pass through the rivers, they will not sweep over you; when you walk through the fire, you will not be burned. The flames will not set you ablaze" (Isaiah 43:1,2).

My favorite hymn is "GOD LEADS HIS DEAR CHILDREN ALONG."

"Some through the water; some thru the flood; some through the fire, but all thru the blood; some thru great trials, but God gives a song; in the night season and all the day long.

Whenever we open our hearts to God's invitation, He proves himself worthy of our trust and commitment. We can, like David of old, have the confidence that God will not call us to confront any enemy that we cannot lay low; nor to bear a cross which we cannot carry, nor to endure a trial that He cannot sustain; nor to do a work which we cannot perform.

John 3:16 is our anchor of hope. We were all dead in sin because of what we did. We are alive in Christ because of what He did. "Thanks be to God for His unspeakable gift." (2 Cor. 9:15).

"Come walk with God, His path is right. He offers love and grace and light. He'll be your guide and show the way; Don't let your feet be led astray. Another path may beckon strong, But offers pleasures that are wrong. So turn away from roads of sin and find the Lord and enter in. Amen."

Max Lucado, in his book, GOD HAS THE LAST WORD writes as follows:

My life is not futile–It has purpose.

My failures are not fatal–God cares for me and forgives.

My death is not final–Christ is the resurrection and the life.

Those who believe in Him will not perish but have everlasting life.

World conditions are not conducive to a positive attitude–wars, corruption in our society, brutalities, rapes, killings and all kinds of frightful behavior dominate the news. Some might be tempted to do what one fellow did; he read that smoking caused cancer so he gave up reading. Therefore, we might reason that if bad news creates fear, we should give up reading. For the bearer of "good news" there is never a time to throw in the towel. I am reminded of the Apostle Paul's words, "I can do all things through Christ who strengthens me" (Philippians 4:13). In keeping with this resolution, I have adopted the following motto: "Whatever I can conceive, if I truly believe, I can surely achieve." (Kineman 1:1).

Chapter 9

PRACTICING THE PRESENCE OF GOD

Someone has registered the following complaint: "I never see my preacher's eyes; There isn't any time, for when he prays he closes his and when he preaches, mine."

Prayer is essential both for the spiritual well being and spiritual growth of the preacher as well as the flock he tends.

In Jesus' Sermon on the Mount, Matthew 6:6–13 he outlines the Where, the When, the How and the What. of effective prayer. As we analyze the Model Prayer, we learn the basics for our prayers.

We should understand: "Thy Kingdom come, thy will be done," is to pray the Father's priority for our lives.

His Kingdom is spiritual in nature (John 18:36)

We cannot enter it except by the new Birth. ((John 3:5).

We must seek first His Kingdom and His righteousness and all things needful will be added to our lives. (Matt. 6:31,32)

Just as we need the Father's Priorities in our lives, we also need His Power to fulfill and manifest these. God's will must be the priority in our lives.

"Not everyone that saith unto me, Lord, Lord, shall enter into the kingdom of heaven; but he that doeth the will of my Father which is in heaven."

THE PRACTICE OF LOVE REASSURES A DOUBTING HEART.

Paul concludes the message on love in 1 Cor. 13 with the declaration: "And now abides faith, hope and love and the greatest of these is love."

When love becomes a deed it does three valuable and important things for us: It assures a doubting heart; It gives boldness and effectiveness to our prayer and gives evidence of a spirit-filled life. The guilty conscience usually arises from at least one of three conditions:

1. When we have committed some gross or repeated sin –bad temper, lustful experience, stealing someone's possessions or good name–"If we confess it, God is faithful to forgive us our sins and to cleanse us from all unrighteousness."

2. There are times when we have a sense of guilt or condemnation because we have been ignored or misunderstood or mistreated. This may produce resentment because a good deed may have been ignored or because our honest motives have been questioned.

3. A third possibility may come from an accusation of the devil: "the trouble with you is that you don't care anymore. You are worthless–you have messed up big time."

What is the remedy? The ground for believing and reassuring ourselves is Romans 8:1. "There is therefore now no condemnation to them which are in Christ Jesus, who walk not after the flesh, but after the Spirit." "His spirit bears witness with our spirit that we are the children of God."(Romans 8:16).

Dr. F. B. Meyer once wrote: "We make a mistake in trying always to clear ourselves. We should be wiser to go straight on, humbly doing the next thing and leaving God to vindicate us". 'He shall bring forth thy righteousness as the light and thy judgment as noonday'."There may come hours in our lives when we shall be misunderstood, slandered, falsely accused. At such times it is very difficult not to act like men around us in the world. They want to appeal to law and force and public opinion. But the believer takes his case into a higher court and lays it before His God.

What about the third condition? When I feel guilty because I have been inactive or disabled? The same thing. Do a deed of love; lift someone up in prayer; write a letter or send a gift–Let love express itself in some way–give of yourself. Be able to laugh at situations and even yourself. "Laughter is the only tranquillizer without any side effects."

THE EXPRESSION OF LOVE BRINGS NOT ONLY A REASSURED HEART BUT ALSO POWER IN PRAYER (1 John 3:21-24).

If our heart does not condemn us, we have confidence before God. The man whose heart does not condemn him is not looking at himself but at the greatness, the majesty, the glory and the power of God. As Paul says in Philippians 3:3 "We... worship God in spirit, and glory in Christ Jesus and put no confidence in the flesh." Putting no confidence in the flesh means we have confidence before God and we will receive from him whatever we ask. Jesus says, "If ye abide in me and my word abides in you, ask what ye will and it shall be done." (John 15:7). The earmarks of true prayer are set forth in this passage:

First, there is the spirit of prayer. We have confidence and boldness before God. 3:21) We do not come before the throne of God on our own merit; We come on Christ' merit.

Second, the purpose of Prayer. It is that you and I are on the receiving end of God's grace. Paul declares in 2 Cor. 8:9: "You know the grace of our Lord Jesus Christ that though he was rich, yet for our sake he became poor, so that by his poverty you might become rich."

Thirdly, the scope of pray "Whatever we ask" (v. 22).Not everything that we might ask., if it is to consume it on our own lusts. Selfish prayer lies outside the realm and purpose of prayer.(James 4:3).

Fourthly, the conditions of prayer. .

Remember the admonition: "If all else fails, read the directions." That applies to our prayers. What are the directions?

BECAUSE WE KEEP HIS COMMANDMENTS AND DO WHAT PLEASES HIM.

Not all of our activities are necessarily pleasing to God. It is not what we do but why we do it that is acceptable to God. Vs. 23 holds the answer. A right motive and a right attitude are essential to answered prayer: "Believe on the name of His son and love one another."

A REASSURED HEART AND POWER IN PRAYER MAKE IT EVIDENT THAT A PERSON IS LIVING A SPIRIT FILLED LIFE .We do not bottle up the Holy Spirit in our lives but allow Him to flow through us to others. To keep Him to ourselves will create stagnation and causes us to become mediocre, dull, sterile and lifeless. Allowing the Spirit to flow through our lives to others, we become refreshed, fragrant and fruitful.

The prayer Jesus taught his Disciples, as recorded in Matthew 6:9-15, is our model. It is brief and to the point. Some have defined prayer by using the acrostic ACTS: Adoration, Confession, Thanksgiving and Supplication.

TYPES OF PRAYER

A. Prayer of Praise–Matthew 6:9; 1 Peter 2:9,10; Psalm 100, 149:1, Psalm 103:1,2.
B. Prayer of Thanksgiving–Ps. 100; 1 Thess. 3:9,10; Philippians 1:3; 1 Timothy 1:12-14.
C. Prayer of Confession–Psalm 51:4; Psalm 32:1-5; 1 John 1:8-10.
D. Prayer of Intercession–1 Timothy 2:1-6; Isaiah 53:12; Ezekiel 22:30,31; Hebrews 7:25.
E. Prayer of Petition–John 15:7; Matthew 7:7-11; Luke 11:5-13.
F. Prayer of Listening–Isaiah 40:31; Psalm 62:5; Psalm 46:10.

SCRIPTURAL ACCOUNTS OF PEOPLE HONORING GOD IN WORSHIP:

A. Bowing heads–Nehemiah 8:6.
B. Bending the knees-Ps. 95:6.
C. The extolling tongue–Ps. 105:2.
D. The singing mouth–Ps. 89:1.
E The clapping hands–Ps. 47:1.
F. The uplifted hands–Ps. 63:4.
G. The shouting voice–Ps. 47:1.
H. The dancing feet–Ps. 149:3.
I. Standing–II Chron. 20:19.
J. Playing instruments–Ps. 150:3-

"We can do more than pray after we have prayed but we cannot do more than pray until we have prayed."

– Lanis E. Kineman

I.   WHAT IS PRAYER?

Prayer springs out of a sense of need both for ourselves and others. This sense of need is joined with a belief that God is a rewarder of them that diligently seek Him (Hebrews 11:6).

II. CONDITIONS FOR EFFECTIVE PRAYER.

God makes His promises that have strings attached, as it were.

A. Pray with pure hearts and clean hands. (Ps. 66:18; 1 Timothy 2:8).
B. We must hear and do God's will. (1 John 3:22; Prov. 28:9).
C. Pray humbly in harmony with His will (Matt. 26:39; 1 John 5:14).
D. Pray fervently and with persistence–(James 5:16b).
E. Pray unselfishly–(James 4:3).
F. Pray in the name of Christ–(John 14: 13-14; 1 Timothy 2:5;

Hebrews 4:14-16; Romans 8:34)

    G. Pray in faith–(Mark 11:24; James 1:5,7' Hebrews 11:6).

    H. Pray with a forgiving spirit–(Matthew 6:12).

III.   THE HOLY SPIRIT ASSISTS IN PRAYER. (Romans 8:26).

IV.   GOD HAS PROMISED ANSWERS TO OUR PRAYERS:

    A. Moses prayed and his prayer saved a nation from death (Exodus 3:14).

    B. Joshua prayed and the sun stood still while his enemies were slain. Hail stones sent from heaven (Joshua 10:10-14).

    C. Hannah prayed and God gave her a son, Samuel (I Samuel 2:9-20)

    D. See 1 Peter 3:12; James 1:5; John 15:7; Luke 11:9,10.

    E. Abraham bargained with God in prayer over the eminent destruction of Sodom & Gomorrah because of their wickedness. There were not even ten righteous people remaining in the cities, so God's judgement prevailed. However, Abraham's nephew, Lot, and his wife and two daughters were warned to flee the city before fire rained down upon the cities. The prayer of Abraham was not answered by God according to his request, but the safety of his nephew, wife and daughters was granted.

(Genesis 19). Ultimately, we may find that God's purpose may not be in granting our specific requests as much as granting our needs. The truth is born out in the oft-quoted lines of a note allegedly found in the pocket of a soldier killed in battle:

"I asked God for strength, that I might achieve;
I was made weak, that I might learn humbly to obey.
I asked for health, that I might do greater things;
I was given poverty that I might be wise.
I asked for power that I might have the praise of men;
I was given weakness, that I might feel the mind of God.
I asked for all things that I might enjoy life;
I got nothing I asked for but everything I had hoped for.
Almost despite myself my unspoken prayers were answered;
I am among men most richly blessed!"

Chapter 10

REWARDS OF A LONG MINISTRY

"The Spirit of the Lord God is upon me; because the Lord hath anointed me to preach good tidings to the meek; he hath sent me to bind up the brokenhearted, to proclaim liberty to the captives, and the opening of the prison to them that are bound; To proclaim the acceptable year of the Lord, and the day of vengeance of our God; to comfort all that mourn: To appoint unto them that mourn in Zion, to give unto them beauty for ashes, the oil of joy for mourning, the garment of praise for the spirit of heaviness; that they might be called trees of righteousness, the planting of the Lord, that he might be glorified." –Isaiah 61:1-3.

The minister of the local church is called upon to wear many hats, but first above all others is preaching. "Go ye into all the world and preach the gospel to every creature." (Mark 16:15).

Having spent twenty-nine years at Bethany Christian Church in Anderson, Indiana, I was often asked why my wife and I chose to stay that long. Facetiously, my answer was something like this:

1. We hate to move.

2. My wife said it was because I was a hard-headed German.

3. Like a successful business executive "I delegated all the responsibility, shifted all the blame and appropriated the credit for myself."

Allow me to break down this subject with an outline recommended by Dr. Holmes, my Philosophy Professor at Butler University several years ago. He suggested to us students that we could rely upon dealing with any subject with three simple points:

1. What is it? 2. What's it worth? 3. How do you get it?

I.   WHAT IS STAYING POWER IN THE MINISTRY?

    A.   Staying power in a local ministry is set forth clearly by the apostle Paul in 2 Timothy 4:1-5. It is in both time frame and purpose.

    B.   Staying power is imperative in view of remembering who our "Commander & Chief" is. He is the Judge of the living and the dead.

The Christian's work must be aimed at pleasing Him, not people. He is the returning Conqueror who motivates us to keep our house in order and our work pleasing to Him. He is King and the day is fast approaching when the Kingdoms of this world will be the Kingdom of our Lord. His return is certain and our efforts will not be in vain.

    C.   Staying power must be evidenced in our preaching: Our message must convey urgency; must be persistent, to correct in love and allow the Word to convict. We must exercise patience–manifesting a spirit that never grows weary, never despairs, never loses faith in human nature and never views man as hopeless and beyond salvation.

II. WHAT'S IT WORTH TRANSLATES INTO "WHAT IS THE VALUE OF A LONG MINISTRY?"

    A.   It allows opportunity for mutual trust on the part of both the congregation and the preacher.

The authority of a servant-leader is not automatically bestowed but earned.

Richard Hutcheson explains leadership as "A function of the relationship between persons, those in charge and those who voluntarily follow. The one thing it cannot do is ignore the constituency."

    B.   It provides "follow-through" for worthy projects begun.
    C.   It produces greater stability within the congregation.
    D.   It enhances the chances of winning more people to Christ from among those the preacher has married and counseled as well as families of those he has buried.
    E.   It enables the preacher to preach over a wide range of Biblical subjects over time.
    F.   It gives the preacher's family a greater sense of security.
    G.   It provides good stewardship of the Lord's money by saving the

high cost of moving.

H. Eliminates the necessity of the preacher having to learn names of church families all over again elsewhere.

I. It enhances the preacher and church's influence in the community.

J. It forces one to deal with arising problems rather than run from them.

III. HOW DO YOU GET IT? TRANSLATES INTO "HOW DO YOU DO IT?"

Leading in ministry involves relationships that must be nurtured on a continuing basis. The preacher has an opportunity to model servant-leadership; however, positive relationships with others must begin with the preacher–his commitment, his priorities and his attitudes.

A. Guidelines for the preacher:
1. Have realistic expectations of yourself. You can't make 12 calls a day on members, make a half dozen prospect calls and spend all your time in the office.
2. Don't neglect a quiet time. Paul, in Philippians 4:4-9 gives the formula for overcoming depression. The peace of God that externalizes itself in rejoicing in the Lord is sandwiched between prayer and positive thinking.
3. Learn contentment. Paul had learned contentment whatever the circumstances through Christ who gave him strength (Philippians 4:12,13.)
4. Laugh a lot. Don't take yourself too seriously.
5. Don't take criticism of your ideas as criticism of you personally.
6. Keep fresh in your preaching by reading, attending Seminars.
7. Take a day off each week and take vacations or mini- trips to get away from the pressures.
8. Live within your income (For your own sake and for the reputation of the church you serve in your community among businesses.)
9. Keep physically fit through proper eating habits and exercise.
10. Give your stress to the Lord (Matthew 11:28-30).
11. Don't run from your problems or pretend they don't exist.
12. Organize your work by dividing jobs into manageable daily segments.

B. Relationships with the church leadership.

1. Cultivate friendships with your leaders–pray, plan and party. Give gifts of appreciation on occasion.
2. Keep lines of communication open. Be liberal with praise, both privately and publically, for tasks well done. Be cautiously critical in private without vindictiveness.
3. Keep things on a positive plane. A negative and critical attitude begets negative and critical people.
4. Keep evangelism a priority.
5. Don't fix blame–fix the problem.
6. Plant ideas for change and growth and let others receive the credit.
7. Delegate responsibility and allow others the freedom to do the job while providing for accountability on their part.
8. Don't make your salary the number one priority when beginning a ministry but be realistic. Have an understanding at the outset about an annual "cost of living" review for adequate salary of yourself and staff members. How do the church leadership wish the image of the minister to be portrayed to the community?
9. Provide a job description for all functional committees.
10. Make long-range plans with the help of the leadership while executing them with congregational endorsement.
11. Encourage flexibility in methodology to enable church growth.
12. Deal with moral problems privately in a spirit of love.
13. Practice the golden rule in all your relationships.

C. Relationship with the church congregation.
1. Love your people, even the unlovable.
2. Make friends out of your enemies. "People are lonely because they build walls instead of bridges."
3. Forgive those who sin against you. Don't hold grudges.
4. Be available to the congregation in sickness, sorrow and other important times in their lives.
5. Be a shepherd to all the flock. Don't play favorites.
6. Be sensitive to criticism but not devastated by it.
7. Avoid exploiting your people for personal favors.
8. Practice what you preach.

D. Relationships with your own family.
1. Spend meaningful time together with your wife and children.
2. Expect no more involvement of your wife in church activities than you do of others.

3. Guard special times for communication between you and your wife.
4. Don't lay the heavy church problems on her, making her vulnerable and defensive in standing up for her husband.
5. Don't set impossible standards for your children. Expect Christian attitudes and behavior, not because they are P. K.'s, but because they are Christians.
6. Make your wife feel important as a part of the team but don't allow her to be dumped on or abused by others.
7. Avoid the lure of greener pastures elsewhere.

E. with the church staff.
1. Choose carefully members of the church staff. The Senior Minister should share in the selection of gifted men or women for specific ministries.
2. Have clearly defined job descriptions so that all may know what is expected of them.
3. Treat them as partners in ministry and give them freedom to fulfill their ministry.
4. Hold regular staff meetings for planning, co-ordinating programs and communications in general. Pray together.
5. Require accountability of all leaders.
6. Avoid rivalry and criticism of one another. Generate a team spirit.
7. Allow for visibility of all staff members in generating their individual feeling of self-worth and congregational expectations.
8. Avoid the paralysis of pride, the listlessness of laziness, the jitters of jealousy, the sin of selfishness and the gangrene of gossip.

F. Relationship with those in the community
1. Be involved and a part of the community as a contributing citizen. Join a civic club, the local ministerial association, the P.T.A. etc.
2. Follow a Code of ministerial Ethics in dealing with other preachers, as well as your predecessor.
3. Make friends of business people and those of other faiths and stand with them on community values.
4. Pay your bills promptly.

The work of a minister is much like the work of a doctor: "It takes more time keeping people alive than it does to introduce new life."

NO TIME TO QUIT

There's a time to part and a time to meet;
There's a time to sleep and a time to eat;
There's a time to work and a time to play'
There's a time to sing and a time to pray;
There's a time that's glad and a time that's blue;
There's a time to plan and a time to do;
There's a time to grin, and show your grit,
But, THERE NEVER WAS A TIME TO QUIT!

– Lanis E. Kineman

THIRTY SUGGESTED MANDATES FOR A LONG MINISTRY

1. Institute change in church traditions and procedures with caution.
2. Train good leadership and equip the saints to carry out the ministry of the church. (Titus 1:5-9)
3. Give attention to detailed planning–short and long range planning
   a. Determine your objectives. State them in writing accurately, briefly and clearly.
   b. Plan necessary activities to achieve objectives.
   c. Organize your program, specifying priorities. "The important is seldom urgent and the urgent is seldom important." –Dwight D. Eisenhower.
   d. Prepare a timetable for completion of each step in your program. Stick to it or revise it–don't drift.
   e. Clarify responsibilities and accountability. In assigning responsibilities, consider ability, availability and dependability of persons involved.
   f. Maintain channels of communication: Keep your associates, superiors, subordinates and others affected properly informed. Avoid Political rhetoric: "I know you believe you understand what you think I said, but I'm not sure you realize that what you heard is not what I meant."
   g. Develop cooperation: Successful achievement largely depends upon groups of people working together for a common goal. Identify what is expected of every individual involved with a job description.
   h. Resolve problems–don't pretend that they don't exist. CLARIFY THE PROBLEM. DEVELOP POSSIBLE SOLUTIONS. SELECT THE BEST SOLUTION. DETERMINE A PLAN OF ACTION AND PUT IT INTO EFFECT.
   i. Give credit where credit is due.

4. Delegate responsibility. It is much easier to do the job of ten people than to train ten people to do the job but the end result will be better for all concerned.

5. Follow through on projects or programs initiated. Success of future proposals depend upon the implementation of previous ones.

6. Tear down barriers and build bridges with people.

7. So live your own personal life above reproach so that if some would defame your character, no one will believe them.

8. Maintain your own personal devotional life in order to overcome depression and rejection by people in whom you have faith.

9. Read good books to keep your preaching fresh, especially the Word of God.

10. Be a good listener to others.

11. Don't show favorites among your people. (Cliques will kill your ministry).

12. Don't leave the impression with people that you know it all and to have the last word on every subject. "Those who think they know it all are amusing to those of us who do."

13. Allow the building committee to do their job. Don't feel that you have to dominate the planning meetings.

14. Make yourself available to people in their real needs–sickness, funerals and weddings. Those needing professional counseling should be referred to a Christian counselor.

15. Safeguard confidences. It's best not to share these even with your wife.

16. Avoid judgmental conclusions about people First impressions can be misleading.

17. Be true to the Word of God. Remember Paul's admonition to Timothy: "Preach the Word; be prepared in season and out of season; correct, rebuke and encourage with great patience and careful instruction." (2 Timothy 4:2).

18. Don't exploit people. The big difference between true Christianity and cultic religion is in the exploitation of people for selfish gain.

19. If you want friends, be one.

20. Be willing to do anything you ask others to do. We all have different gifts but small, menial tasks should not be beneath the preacher. Sometimes just getting our hands dirty can break down artificial barriers between us and others.

21. Use personal criticism of yourself constructively. Ignore negative and senseless criticism but be willing to profit from constructive criticism. Most of our negative critics are those who don't do anything themselves. (Most churches are made up of three groups of people:

(1)Those who don't know what's happening; (2) Those who just watch what 's happening; (3) Those who make things happen.

22. Don't be jealous of your predecessor, successor or co-laborer in ministry.

23. Maintain proper hygiene and neat appearance (especially in the pulpit).

24. Pay your debts promptly.

25. Love your wife, if you have one. This will be the best thing you can do for your children as a role model. Though you may not have any, other children will be observing.

26. Avoid the laziness like the plague. Lead a well disciplined life.

27. A healthy attitude is as important if not more so than ability and action.

28. No person can be proficient in all areas of ministry. While you can't do everything, surround yourself with individuals who can do the job.

29. STAY PUT. Avoid the temptation of thinking the grass is greener on the other side of the fence. Don't make major decisions when you are depressed. Longer ministries have been proven to be more fruitful.

30. Be a good steward. The first consideration of a pastorate should not be money. Honesty, frugality and contentment should be watchwords relating to the management of personal finances.

TESTIMONIES OF OTHERS WITH LONG MINISTRIES

In preparing this dissertation on Ministry, I sent out requests to preachers who have led successful, long ministries at one location. The following are responses received.

The first came from Don Wilson, Senior minister of the large Christ Church of the Valley in Peoria, Arizona. This congregation has grown numerically over the years to become among the largest Christian Churches in the Nation in the 1970s with ties to the Restoration Movement. He submitted the following:

"One of the biggest rewards is seeing people's lives change over a long period. Often in shorter ministries we do not get to see significant life changes. A longer ministry allows you to observe people as they go through many life changes and struggles which can really develop their character."

"Another reward of a long term ministry is watching generational conversions. You begin your ministry with a couple, you baptize their children, you marry their children and then you get to baptize their grandchildren. Very few Christians today are seeing the 2nd and 3rd generation continue to follow in their parents faith. It is a joy to see strong families that transfer their faith to their children."

"I would also mention a couple of challenges in a long term ministry:

One is the continual growth that the pastor must have. After you preach in the same church for many years, your long term members already know your stories, your life and your favorite passages and sayings. You have to continually grow or they will no longer be challenged by your preaching.

"A second adjustment is that you have to make personal changes in your life and priorities over a long term ministry. What you can do with little children vs. what you can do when you have teenagers vs. what you can do as an empty nest pastor is very different. You have to be flexible with your leadership style and your schedule or it will cause lost of problems in your marriage and in your ministry."

The following paragraphs include excerpts from a few other successful ministers who responded to my request.

Wayne Smith, former Senior Minister of Southland Christian Church, Lexington, Kentucky was known in his ministry as the Preacher's Preacher. His church was among the largest churches of our brotherhood during his long ministry. He and I were good friends over the years and joined in mutual projects for church growth. We were friendly rivals of different Bible Colleges but supportive of each other's ministry. Wayne's response was:

1. Stability for the church family. "I ministered forty years with the Southland Christian Church, Lexington, Kentucky, a city of 250,000. Frequent change adversely affects the institution."
2. Stability for the minister's family.
3. Deep relationship with the church that earns their trust.
4. Clout in the community. " When the local newspaper had a question they called me first because they knew my name. The same was true with television news and local radio talk shows. I have been honored many times and have been asked to speak to various churches and a number of civic groups because they respect a name that survives the passing of time."
5 Longevity that attracts people of other fellowships. A common expression was: "I'm coming to Southland when our preacher leaves."
6. Balanced preaching with creativity.... "It takes time after you sow to reap a crop The average minister leaving after three or four years may not see the result of his labors."
7. "Seeing one's goals fulfilled. The church was planted by Broadway Christian Church contributing 93 adults. The first Sunday saw 125...Growth

continued over the years" . . . . Wayne retired in 1996. At that time attendance was 10,000 each weekend in five services,

8. "A closer kinship with Elders and Deacons because they joined under the preacher's leadership."

9. "Perks! These normally come with a long ministry. I have been greatly blessed with many perks including a new Cadillac and a new Lincoln Town Car."

10. Media Exposure. "Southland has purchased an hour on Sunday morning on an ABC-TV station for the past 23 years. Its viewing audience is 50,000."

Bob Russell, former minister of the Southeast Christian Church, Louisville, KY, among the largest of the Restoration Churches in our Brotherhood, gave a similar testimony:

1. The long term ministry gave stability to his family by remaining put over the years.

2. It garnered respect from the community through the church outreach and involvement in community affairs.

3. It made possible knowing his people over a long period and growing to love them and be loved by them.

4. It helped to deepen the perspective of God's plan of redemption for all people.

5. It, most of all, helped him to be patient with people throughout his ministry.

His long-term ministry of changing locations three times to enable growth to take place, build a support staff and maintain a Scriptural position all was made possible by a long ministry in a metropolitan city.

REWARDS OF A LONG MINISTRY OF THE CAPITAL AREA CHRISTIAN CHURCH IN MECHANICSBURG, PA.

Don Hamilton, related an account of the growth of the his congregation over the period of thirty years in an area of few other Christian Churches. He writes: "The church is presently located on a fifty-three acre campus that is a community park, dedicated to people with special needs. Fifty-one community groups use the campus at this writing. A new campus is being launched in the Harrisburg area. A tree has not fulfilled its destiny until it has born other trees, not just its own fruit." He continues: "The benefits of staying put are numerous: I've seen my children grow up with deep friendships and a wonderful extended family. I've seen the church grow from 30/40 people to 750. I've seen the third generation now venture into the world and into vocational ministry. I've raised up leader after leader and enjoyed the fruit of their ministry. I've seen churches planted and a movement gain momentum. I've witnessed the results of generational projects and completed new horizons. I've grown up and performed my ministry in full view of three, almost four generations. Each one impacted my life for the better. Now, I'm learning from these kids whose parents I know so well and together, we're still growing a great church and expanding the Kingdom. Statistics tell us that most pastors will move from one church to another through the life of their ministry. Yet, study after study reveals that the long-term ministry bears the most fruit. So, maybe we should encourage young men and women to start a new thing or renew an old thing and then grow up and serve long enough to see an orchard." (Don was baptized during my long ministry at Bethany Christian Church. He was recruited to Christian service by James Harless, one of Bethany's earliest of forty three Timothies and youth minister at the Southern Heights Christian Church in Anderson, planted by Bethany. Church plants and Timothies are often spawned by long ministries.

REWARDS OF MY LONG MINISTRY AT BETHANY CHRISTIAN CHURCH

1. It gave opportunity to bring stability to the leadership and church growth. (It takes about three to four years to develop trust and to experience change)

2. It enabled me to become known and accepted in the community.

3. It allowed the time needed to make and carry out church programs that attracted non-Christians to the services and activities.

4. It gave continuity to the evangelistic outreach of the church in the community. Winning people to the Lord sometimes takes several years.

5. Being established and known in the community enabled me to join forces with other preachers and church leaders for a voice in community affairs.

6. Longer exposure to young people blessed me to influence them for specialized Christian service. (We had forty-three recruits for missionary endeavors and Christian ministry.)

7. It afforded an opportunity to establish life-long friends.

8. It enabled us to establish outreach programs both locally and Internationally.

9. It gave stability to our four children, blessing them to grow up and be involved in the local schools and organizations.

10. Before retirement we were blessed by the gift of our lovely house that had been privileged to call home over the years.

ADDITIONAL THOUGHTS

1. A long ministry is a productive ministry.

2. A long ministry provides the minister with genuine friendships—not mere acquaintances.

3. A long ministry offers leadership to the community where you live.

4. A long ministry strengthens the family. The children are not changing schools every few years.

5. A long ministry enables the church members to minister to the minister as well as you ministering to them.

6. A long ministry will provide acceptance to your personality, habits and dedication, whether it be dress patterns, humor, etc.

7. A long ministry provides friendship with the other ministers of the brotherhood in the area where you preach. Your witness is really more appreciated by long term associations.

8. A long ministry enables you to develop good work habits and establish a daily routine.

9. A long ministry challenges you to lead with relevant and productive ideas.

10. A long ministry gives you the right to be heard. The right to be heard and respected must be earned.

– Glen Wheeler

Chapter 11

RUNNING THE COURSE / KEEPING THE FAITH

The apostle Paul delivered a final charge to young Timothy in the following solemn words with a request for him to come to him in his hour of need:

> "For I am now ready to be offered, and the time of my departure is at hand. I have fought a good fight, I have finished my course, I have kept the faith: Henceforth there is laid up for me a crown of righteousness, which the Lord, the righteous judge, shall give me at that day: and not to me only, but unto all them also that love his appearing." (2 Timothy 4:6-8).

These words have to resonate to every faithful servant of the Lord who has spent a lifetime of laying his all on the altar of service for the Lord's work. The question that must be asked of all who commit to preaching the Good News of Jesus Christ is contained in the familiar hymn, " Is Your All on the Altar?" By Elisha A. Hoffman:

> You have longed for sweet peace, and for faith to increase,
> And have earnestly, fervently prayed;
> But you cannot have rest or be perfectly blest
> Until all on the altar is laid.
> Who can tell all the love He will send from above,
> And how happy our hearts will be made,
> Of the fellowship sweet we shall share at His feet,
> When our all on the altar is laid.
>
> Is your all on the altar of sacrifice laid?

Your heart, does the Spirit control?
You can only be blest and have peace and sweet rest,
As you yield Him your body and soul.

When a minister was introduced the first Sunday of his ministry, he was pleasantly surprised to be greeted with sustained applause. Thanking them, he said that when there is an applause at the beginning of a ministry, that's faith. When there is applause at the middle of the ministry, that's hope. When there is applause at the end of a ministry, that's charity. Paul mentioned faith, hope and charity. He concluded–the greatest of these is charity.

Having formally retired a second time in June, 2011, from the position of Minister to Seniors, and rounding out 64 years of ministry since my ordination in 1946, I am now ready to make some final observations and challenges to all who are committed to Christian ministry

I have attempted, in this writing, to review some experiences and extend some challenges and reflect on the rewards of ministry.

In recent years, I have reflected on the various stages through which I have passed in my commitment to the Lord.

First, as a young preacher, fresh out of Bible College I was TIRELESS. I mistakenly thought I could turn the world upside down for Christ. There was no sacrifice too great and no task too small for me to do in my commitment to Him. After serving many long hours and wearing many hats I became TIRED. Thus, adjustments had to be made and approaches to ministry had to undergo some changes. Undertaking too many projects, study and sermon preparation suffered and my long sermons became TIRESOME both to me and the congregation. After twenty-nine years as the preaching minister at Anderson, Indiana and yearning for some personal free time, I RETIRED. This seemed to work for a very short time but I soon learned that preachers don't retire, they just go out to pastor. With some unexpected developments in family affairs, my wife, Kathryn, and I ended up in Chandler, Arizona ministering to Seniors under the leadership of Roger Storms, preaching minister. I found myself being

RETREADED for continued ministry.

This new venture took me from Chandler to Sun City; then to Wickenburg and finally to Paseo Verde Christian church in Peoria, Arizona. Having retired a second time in June, 2011, Nancy and I became a part of the fellowship of Sun City West Christian Church, Dr. Wayne Dykstra, preaching minister.

I have had three different Christian wives at my side over these years: I was blessed with 46 years with my first wife, Kathryn Turnbull Kineman and the mother of my four children. Having lost her in death, I was blessed with a second companion in ministry, Vanda Rodgers for 6 ½ years. The Lord brought my present wife, Nancy Norton and me together at Christ Church of the Valley in Peoria, Az. We have labored together for seven years at this writing. She has been a Christian helpmeet par-excellent.

In my speaking engagements, I used to refer to Kathryn as the love of my life and that we met and dated on the campus of Johnson Bible College. I bragged that I could have married any girl on campus that I pleased; it just happened that she was the only one I pleased. One of the busiest weeks of our lives was at Commencement time at the College on a Monday, May 31st, 1948. We traveled to Paterson, N. J. where her preacher father, Wm. Turnbull, ordained her for ministry on Wednesday. We tied the knot on Saturday, June 5th in a beautiful church wedding. Over the years, she was a tireless but proud minister's wife and was once referred to by the elders at Bethany as an angel because "She was always up in the air harping about something."

The Scripture verse submitted by Brother Wayne Smith best describes our own ministries: "He who refreshes others will be himself refreshed." (Proverbs 11:25).

Sometimes we come to life's crossroads,
And view what we think is the end,
But God has a much wider vision.
He knows it's only a bend.

The road will go on and get smoother,
And after we've stopped for a rest,
The path that lies beyond us,
Is often the path that is best.

So rest, relax and grow stronger
Let go and let God share your load.
Have faith in a brighter tomorrow
You've come to a bend in the road.

My passion for Christian Ministry would not be complete without a challenge to those who would follow in the footsteps of all who have gone before: "Therefore, my beloved brethren, be ye steadfast, unmoveable, always abounding in the work of the Lord, forasmuch as ye know that your labour is not in vain in the Lord." (1 Cor. 15:58). (KJV).

The purpose of this book has been a Celebration of Praise for Ministry. I make no apology for the contents. I trust that it will be a blessing to those desiring to do the Lord's will in their lives, unlike the pessimistic beatitude: "Blessed is the man who has nothing to say and cannot be persuaded to say it." Preaching should be bold, unapologetic, loving, scriptural and urgent.

"But thanks be to God, which giveth us the victory through our Lord Jesus Christ. Therefore, my beloved brethren, be ye steadfast, unmoveable, always abounding in the work of the Lord, forasmuch as ye know that your labour is not in vain in the Lord."- 1 Cor. 16:57, 58.

Taking a look at the past and REFLECTING upon it, RENEWING our faith in the present while RESOLVING to stand firm in the future can be both helpful and refreshing. An uncommon faith in Christ means taking some risks:

> Half the wrecks upon life's ocean,
> If some star had been their guide;
> Would have safely reached the harbor
> Instead, drifted with the tide.
> If the ship doesn't have a port, it won't dock.

On the flyleaf of her favorite Bible, my wife of 46 years had inscribed the following words: "When this passing world is done; When has sunk yon glowing sun; When we stand with Christ in glory, Looking o'er life's finished story, Then, Lord shall I fully know; Not 'till then how much I owe."

Charles Gabriel wrote the lyrics to a favorite hymn:

"When all my labors and trials are o'er
And I am safe on that beautiful shore,
Just to be near the dear Lord I adore,
Will through the ages be glory for me.
O that will be, glory for me, glory for me,
Glory for me, When by his grace I shall look on his face.
That will be glory, be glory for me."

Our mission as Christians is to

> Stand firm
> Work tirelessly
> Expect results.

"Stand firm, brothers. Let nothing move you. Always give yourselves fully to the work of the Lord, because you know that your labor is not in vain." (1 Corinthians 15:57-58).

Chapter 12

GROWING OLD GRACEFULLY

Solomon, blessed of the Lord with both wealth and wisdom declared the following: "To everything there is a season, and a time to every purpose under the heaven; A time to be born and a time to die;" (Ecclesiastes 3:1,2a)

In the book of Proverbs, He weighs in on man's moral values, declaring: "A good name is rather to be chosen than great riches, and loving favour rather than silver and gold." (Proverbs 22:1).

The apostle Paul refers to the seasons of life in 2 Corinthians 4:15-18.

"For all things are for your sakes, that the abundant grace might through the thanksgiving of many redound to the glory of God. For which cause we faint not; but though our outward man perish, yet the inward man is renewed day by day. For our light affliction, which is but for a moment, worketh for us a far more exceeding and eternal weight of glory; While we look not at the things which are seen: for the things which are seen are temporal; but the things which are not seen are eternal."

In the final analysis it's not how much wealth we have accumulated to leave for others or whether our name has been displayed in lights for all to see; what really counts is receiving the commendation of our Lord: "Well done thou good and faithful servant; thou hast been faithful over a few things, I will make thee ruler over many things: enter thou into the joy of thy Lord." (Matthew 25:21b). This commendation was communicated by the Master to the servant who had been entrusted with five talents and had doubled what he had received. The sweetest words that any of us could hope to hear at the conclusion of our earthly life is such a commendation from the Lord of the Universe. Lip service or flimsy excuses will not stand in that hour. Only what is done out of concern for the will of God will endure.

PERFORMANCE is a prerequisite to our Lord's commendation. Jesus said, "Not everyone who says to me, 'Lord, Lord' will enter the kingdom of heaven, but only he who does the will of my Father who is in heaven." (Matt. 7:21). Too many of us are like the deacon who prayed: "Use me, O Lord, in the work – especially in an advisory capacity."

PERSEVERANCE is also needful both in doing of the Lord's will and in the use of our spiritual gifts for His glory. With the grandstand filled with faithful performers of the past, the Hebrews writer exhorts us to throw off any thing that would impede our progress and ". . . run with perseverance the race marked out for us." (Hebrews 12:1b).

PERFECTION is most certainly the end goal. Sinlessness of character is an elusive dream. Righteousness comes by faith in Christ. Perfection as our goal is rightly translated "maturity". James warns us that the " trying of our faith worketh patience". He admonishes, "But let patience have her perfect work, that ye may be perfect and entire, wanting nothing." (James 2:4). The NIV translates this verse: "Perseverance must finish its work so that you may be mature and complete, not lacking anything." Let us endeavor to grow up unto Christ, that, at the end of our earthly journey, we may be commended by Him.

As we enter into the sunset years of our lives, we have to face the decision: Will we be a burden to others or a blessing? Someone has shared the following:

THE SECRET OF LIVING:

The secret of living is learning to pray,
It's asking our Father for strength for the day!
It's trusting completely that His boundless grace
Will overcome care and each problem we face!
It's walking by faith every mile that we plod,
And knowing our prayers bring us closer to God.

"We cannot see nor can we know, the meaning of life's tears;
But we can trust and we can hope which conquers all our fears.
A misty veil hides what's ahead, but we can trust the one who said,
"Fear not, have faith, be not afraid."

– *Lanis E. Kineman*

Just for today–

I will try to live through this day only and not tackle all of life's problems at once. I can do something for twelve hours that would appall me if I felt that I had to keep it up for a life time.

Just for today–

I will be happy. This assumes to be true what Abraham Lincoln once said, that "Most folks are as happy as they make up their minds to be.

Just for today–

I will try to strengthen my mind. I will study. I will learn something useful. I will not be a mental loafer. I will read something that requires effort, thought and concentration.

Just for today–

I will exercise my soul in three ways:

I will do somebody a good turn and not get found out doing it.

If anybody knows of it, it will not count.

I will do at least two things I don't want to do–just for exercise. I will not show anyone that my feelings are hurt; they may be hurt, but today I will not show it.

Just for today–

I will be agreeable. I will look as well as I can, dress becomingly, talk low, act courteously, criticize not one bit, not find fault with anything and not try to improve or regulate anybody except myself.

Just for today---

I will have a program. I may not follow it exactly but I will have it. I will save myself from two pests: hurry and indecision.

Just for today–

I will have a quiet half hour all by myself and relax. During this half hour, sometime, I will try to get a better perspective of my life.

Just for today–

I will be unafraid; especially I will not be afraid to enjoy what is beautiful and believe that as I give to the world, so the world will give back to me.

Consider some of the favorite quotes of all times:

He drew a circle that shut me out–
Heretic, rebel, a thing to flout;
But love and I had the wit to win;
We drew a circle that took him in.

– Edwin Markham

A bell is not a bell till you ring it.
A song is not a song until you sing it.
Love in your heart is not put there to stay;
Love is not love 'till you give it away.

– James W. Russell

Take yesterday's worries and sort them all out
And you'll wonder whatever you worried about;
Look back at the cares that once furrowed your brow–
I fancy you'll smile at most of them now.
They seemed terrible then, but they really were not;
For once out of the woods, all the fears are forgot.

– Author unknown

For a happy life, three things are necessary!
1. Something to hope for.
2. Something to do.
3. Someone to love.
    – William Barclay

LESSONS FROM THE CARPENTER

Once upon a time two brothers who lived on adjoining farms fell into conflict. It was their first serious rift in 40 years of farming side-by-side, sharing machinery and trading labor and goods as needed, without a hitch. Then the long collaboration fell apart. It began with a small misunderstanding and it grew into a major difference. Finally, it exploded into an exchange of bitter words, followed by weeks of silence.

One morning, there was knock on John's door. He opened it to find a man with a carpenter's toolbox. "I'm looking for a few days' work" he said. "Perhaps you would have a few small jobs here and there I could help with."

"Could I help you?"

"Yes," said the older brother. "I do have a job for you. Look across the creek at that farm. That's my neighbor. In fact, he's my younger brother! Last week, there was a meadow between us. He recently took his bulldozer to the river levee, and now there is a creek between us." "Well, he may have done this to spite me, but I'll do him one better. See that pile of lumber by the barn? I want you to build me a fence. An eight-foot fence–so I won't need to see his place or his face anymore."

The carpenter said, "I think I understand the situation. Show me the nails and the post-hole digger and I'll be able to do a job that pleases you."

The older brother had to go to town, so he helped the carpenter get the materials ready and then he was off for the day. The carpenter worked hard all that day–measuring, sawing and nailing.

About sunset, when the farmer returned, the carpenter had just finished his job. The farmer's eyes opened wide and his jaw dropped. There was no fence there at all. It was a bridge that stretched from one side of the creek to the other! A fine piece of work, with handrails and all.! And, the neighbor, his younger brother was coming toward them, his hand outstretched . . . "You are quite a fellow to build this bridge. After all I've said and done." The two brothers stood at each end of the bridge and then they met in the middle, taking each other's hand. They turned to see the carpenter hoist his toolbox onto his shoulder. "No wait! Stay a few days. I've a lot of other projects for you,: said the older brother. "I'd love to stay on," the carpenter said, "but I have many more bridges to build."

The moral of this story is:

1. God won't ask what kind of car you drove, but He'll ask how many people you helped get where they needed to go.
2. God won't ask the square footage of your house, but He'll ask how many people you welcomed into your home.
3. God won't ask about the clothes you had in your closet, but He'll ask how many you helped to clothe.
4. God won't ask how many friends you had, but He'll ask how many people to whom you were a friend.
5. God won't ask in what neighborhood you lived, but He'll ask how you treated your neighbors.
6. God won't ask about the color of your skin, but he'll ask about the content of your character.
7. God won't ask why it took you so long to seek Salvation, but He'll lovingly take you to your mansion in heaven and not to the gates of Hell.

– Copied from the *Carlisle Christian Newsletter*, Carlisle, Ky.

A RETIRED PREACHER'S REFLECTION ON LIFE

DRINKING FROM THE SAUCER

I've never made a fortune and it's probably too late now,
I don't worry about that much; I'm happy anyhow.

And as I go along life's way, I'm reaping better than I sowed,
I'm drinking from the saucer, 'cause my cup has overflowed.'

Haven't got a lot of riches and sometimes the going's tough;
But I've got loving ones around me and that makes me rich enough.

I thank God for his blessings, and the mercies He's bestowed.
I'm drinking from my saucer, 'cause my cup has overflowed.'

O, remember times when things went wrong, My faith wore
somewhat thin;
But all at once the dark clouds broke and the sun peeped through
again.

So Lord, help me not to gripe about the tough rows that I've hoed,
I'm drinking from my saucer, 'cause my cup has overflowed.'

If God gives me strength and courage, when the way grows steep and
rough;
I'll not ask for other blessings, I'm already blessed enough.

And may I never be too busy, to help others bear their loads;
Then I'll keep drinking from my saucer, 'cause my cup has
overflowed.'

– Author Unknown

41473075R00068

Made in the USA
Charleston, SC
29 April 2015